5-Ingredients Plant Based Diet Cookbook

4 Books in 1: The Complete Guide to Plant Based Foods for Healthy Weight Loss with 200+ Quick, Easy & Delicious Recipes Full of Nutrients

Frank Smith

Plant Based Diet Cookbook for Beginners 2021

The Complete Guide to Plant Based Foods for Healthy Weight Loss with Quick, Easy & Delicious Recipes

Frank Smith

Table Of Contents

Breakfasts

1 A Toast to Remember

Preparation time: 10 minutes Cooking time: 15 minutes
Servings: 4
Ingredients:

1 can, black beansPinch, sea salt

2 pieces, whole-wheat toast

¼ teaspoon, chipotle spicePinch, black pepper
1 teaspoon, garlic powder1 freshly juiced lime
1 freshly diced avocado

¼ cup, corn

3 tablespoons, finely diced onion

½ freshly diced tomatoFresh cilantro Directions:
Mix the chipotle spice with the beans, salt, garlic powder,
andpepper. Stir in the lime juice.

Boil all of these until you have a thick and starchy mix.

In a bowl, mix the corn, tomato, avocado, red onion, cilantro, and juice from the rest of the lime. Add some pepper and salt.

Toast the bread and first spread the black bean mixture followed by the avocado mix.

Take a bite of wholesome goodness!

Nutrition: Calories: 290, Fats 9 g, Carbohydrates 44 g, Proteins 12 g

2 Tasty Panini

Preparation time: 5 minutes Cooking time: 0 minutes Serving: 1
Ingredients:

¼ cup, hot water

1 tablespoon, cinnamon

¼ cup, raisins

2 teaspoons, cacao powder1 ripe banana
2 slices, whole-grain bread

¼ cup, natural peanut butterDirections:
In a bowl, mix the cinnamon, hot water, raisins, and cacao powder.

Spread the peanut butter on the bread.

Cut the bananas and put them on the toast.

Mix the raisin mixture in a blender and spread it on the sandwich.

Nutrition: Calories: 850, Fats 34 g, Carbohydrates 112 g, Proteins 27g

3 Tasty Oatmeal and Carrot Cake

Preparation time: 10 minutes Cooking time: 10 minutes
Serving: 1
Ingredients:

1 cup, water

½ teaspoon, cinnamon1 cup, rolled oats
Salt

¼ cup, raisins

½ cup, shredded carrots1 cup, non-dairy milk
¼ teaspoon, allspice

½ teaspoon, vanilla extractToppings:
¼ cup, chopped walnuts

2 tablespoons, maple syrup

2 tablespoons, shredded coconutDirections:
Put a small pot on low heat and bring the non-dairy
milk, oats, and

water to a simmer.

Now, add the carrots, vanilla extract, raisins, salt,
cinnamon and allspice. You need to simmer all of the
ingredients, but do not forget

to stir them. You will know that they are ready when the
liquid is fully absorbed into all of the ingredients (in about
7-10 minutes).

Transfer the thickened dish to bowls. You can drizzle some maple syrup on top or top them with coconut or walnuts.

Nutrition: Calories: 210, Fats 11.48 g, Carbohydrates 10.37 g,

Proteins 3.8 g

4 Whole Grain Protein Bowl

Preparation time: 10 mCooking time: 0 m Ingredients:

1 sliced banana

1/3 cup whole grains (like millet, couscous, quinoa, oat groats, etc.)cooked in 2/3 cup water

1 tablespoon nut butter

2 tablespoons dried goji berries

1 tablespoon raw sweetener (or throw in some dates or raisins)3 tablespoons dried coconut chunks
1 tablespoon cacao nibsDirections:
Throw it all together and eat!

5 Berry Beetsicle Smoothie

Preparation time: 3 minutes Cooking time: 0minutes
Servings: 1
Ingredients

½ Cup peeled and diced beets

½ Cup frozen raspberries1 frozen banana
1 tablespoon maple syrup

1 cup unsweetened soy or almond milkDirections
Combine all the Ingredients in a blender and blend until smooth.

6 Blueberry Oat Muffins

Preparation time: 10 minutes Cooking time: 20 minutes Servings: 12 mufins Ingredients

2 tablespoons coconut oil or vegan margarine, melted, plus more forpreparing the muffin tin

1 cup quick-cooking oats or instant oats 1 cup boiling water

½ Cup nondairy milk

¼ Cup ground flaxseed

1 teaspoon vanilla extract

1 teaspoon apple cider vinegar1½ cups whole-grain flour ½ Cup brown sugar

2 teaspoons baking sodaPinch salt

1 cup blueberriesDirections
Preheat the oven to 400°f.

Coat a muffin tin with coconut oil, line with paper muffin cups, or usea nonstick tin.

In a large bowl, combine the oats and boiling water. Stir so the oats soften. Add the coconut oil, milk, flaxseed, vanilla, and vinegar and stir to combine. Add the flour, sugar, baking soda, and salt. Stir until just combined. Gently fold in the blueberries. Scoop the muffin mixture into the prepared tin, about ⅓ cup for each muffin.

Bake for 20 to 25 minutes, until slightly browned on top

and springy to the touch. Let cool for about 10 minutes. Run a dinner knife around the inside of each cup to loosen, then tilt the muffins on their sides in the muffin wells so air gets underneath. These keep in an airtight container in the refrigerator for up to 1 week or in the freezer indefinitely.

Nutrition (1muffin): calories: 174; protein: 5g; total fat: 3g; saturated fat:2g; carbohydrates: 33g; fiber: 4g

7 Quinoa Applesauce Muffins

Preparation time: 10 minutes Cooking time: 15 minutes
Servings: 5
Ingredients

2 tablespoons coconut oil or margarine, melted, plus more forcoating the muffin tin

¼ Cup ground flaxseed

½ Cup water

2 cups unsweetened applesauce

½ Cup brown sugar

1 teaspoon apple cider vinegar2½ cups whole-grain flour
1½ cups cooked quinoa 2 teaspoons baking soda Pinch salt
½ Cup dried cranberries or raisinsDirections
Preheat the oven to 400°f.

Coat a muffin tin with coconut oil, line with paper muffin cups, or use a nonstick tin. In a large bowl, stir together the flaxseed and water. Add the applesauce, sugar, coconut oil, and vinegar. Stir to combine. Add the flour, quinoa, baking soda, and salt, stirring until just

combined. Gently fold in the cranberries without stirring too much. Scoop the muffin mixture into the prepared tin, about ⅓ cup for each muffin.

Bake for 15 to 20 minutes, until slightly browned on top

and springy to the touch. Let cool for about 10 minutes. Run a dinner knife around the inside of each cup to loosen, then tilt the muffins on their sides in the muffin wells so air gets underneath. These keep in an airtight container in the refrigerator for up to 1 week or in the freezer indefinitely.

Per serving(1muffin): calories: 387; protein: 7g; total fat: 5g; saturated fat: 2g; carbohydrates: 57g; fiber: 8g

8 Yogurt with Cucumber

Preparation Time: 5 minutes Cooking Time: 0 minute
Serving: 1
Ingredients:

1 cup soy yogurt

½ cucumber, diced

¼ teaspoon lemon zest

¼ teaspoon freshly squeezed lemon juiceSalt to taste
Chopped mint leavesDirections:
Put all the ingredients in a glass jar with lid. Refrigerate
overnight or up to 2 days.
Nutrition: Calories: 164 fat: 3.9g Saturated fat: 2.5g
Cholesterol:

15mg   Sodium: 319mg   Potassium: 683mg
Carbohydrates: 19.1gFiber: 0.6g Sugar: 18g Protein: 13.3g

9 Breakfast Casserole

Preparation: 20 minutesCooking: 43 minutes Servings: 6
Ingredients:

10 oz. spinach

9 oz. artichoke hearts 2 cloves garlic, minced
¾ cup sun-dried tomatoes, chopped

½ teaspoon red pepper flakes1 teaspoon lemon zest
1 tablespoon olive oil2 cups almond milk
1 cup vegan cheese, crumbled

8 cups whole wheat bread, choppedDirections:
Squeeze the spinach to release the liquid. Add the spinach to a bowl.
Stir in the artichoke hearts.

In a pan over low heat, cook the garlic, tomatoes, red pepper andlemon zest in oil for 3 minutes.
Add the spinach and artichokes.Remove from heat.
Transfer to a baking pan.

Stir in the spinach mixture and bread. Let sit for 30 minutes.Bake in the oven at 350 degrees F for 40 minutes.
Store in a food container and refrigerate.
Reheat before serving.
Nutrition: Calories: 277 fat: 9.9g Saturated fat: 4.5g Cholesterol: 136mg Sodium: 498mg Potassium: 542mg Carbohydrates: 30.5g Fiber: 4.8g Sugar: 6g Protein: 14.4g

10 Breakfast Parfait Popsicles

Preparation time: 10 minutes Cooking time: 0 minutes
Servings: 02
Ingredients:

1 cup soy yogurt1 cup berries
1 cup granola

Directions:

In a popsicle mold, divide the berries.

Add yogurt to the molds and gently mix the berries using a stick. Sprinkle granola on top and place the popsicle sticks in the mixture.Freeze overnight.
Serve.

Nutrition: Calories 135 Total Fat 2 g Saturated Fat 1 g Cholesterol 2

mg Sodium 17 mg Total Carbs 33 g Fiber 1 g Sugar 13 g Protein 2g

Soups, Salads, and Sides

11 Tomato Pumpkin Soup

Preparation time: 25 minutes Cooking time: 15 minutes
Servings: 4
Ingredients:

1 cups pumpkin, diced 1/2 cup tomato, chopped 1/2 cup
onion, chopped 1 1/2 tsp curry powder 1/2 tsp paprika
2 cups vegetable stock 1 tsp olive oil
1/2 tsp garlic, minced Directions:

In a saucepan, add oil, garlic, and onion and sauté for
3 minutes over medium heat.

Add remaining ingredients into the saucepan and bring to
boil. Reduce heat and cover and simmer for 10 minutes.
Puree the soup using a blender until smooth.

Stir well and serve warm.

Nutrition: calories 70; fat 2.7 g; carbohydrates 13.8 g;

sugar 6.3 g;

protein 1.9 g; cholesterol 0 mg

12 Cauliflower Spinach Soup

Preparation time: 45 minutes Cooking time: 25 minutes
Servings: 5
Ingredients:

1/2 cup unsweetened coconut milk 5 oz fresh spinach, chopped
5 watercress, chopped

8 cups vegetable stock 1 lb cauliflower, choppedSalt
Directions:

Add stock and cauliflower in a large saucepan and bring to boil overmedium heat for 15 minutes.

Add spinach and watercress and cook for another 10 minutes. Remove from heat and puree the soup using a blender until smooth. Add coconut milk and stir well. Season with salt.
Stir well and serve hot.

Nutrition: calories 153; fat 8.3 g; carbohydrates 8.7 g; sugar 4.3 g;

protein 11.9 g; cholesterol 0 mg

13 Avocado Mint Soup

Preparation time: 10 minutes Cooking time: 10 minutes Servings: 2
Ingredients:

1 medium avocado, peeled, pitted, and cut into pieces 1 cup coconut milk

2 romaine lettuce leaves

20 fresh mint leaves 1 tbsp fresh lime juice 1/8 tsp salt
Directions:

Add all ingredients into the blender and blend until smooth. Soupshould be thick not as a puree.

Pour into the serving bowls and place in the refrigerator for 10minutes.

Stir well and serve chilled.

Nutrition: calories 268; fat 25.6 g; carbohydrates 10.2 g; sugar 0.6 g;

protein 2.7 g; cholesterol 0 mg

Entrées

14 Cauliflower Popcorn

Preparation time: 1 day and 1 hourCooking time: 1 day
Servings: 2

Ingredients:

¼ cup sun-dried tomatoes

¾ cup dates

2 heads cauliflower

½ cup water

2 tablespoons raw tahini

1 tablespoon apple cider vinegar 2 teaspoons onion
powder
2 teaspoons garlic powder

1 teaspoon ground cayenne pepper

2 tablespoons nutritional yeast (optional)Directions:

Cover the sun-dried tomatoes warm water and let them soak for anhour.

If the dates are not soft and fresh, soak them in warm water for anhour in another bowl.

Cut the cauliflower in very small, bite-sized pieces then set aside.

Put the drained tomatoes and dates in a blender along with the water, tahini, apple cider vinegar, onion powder, garlic powder,

cayenne pepper, nutritional yeast and turmeric. Blend into a thick, smooth consistency.

Pour this mixture into the bowl, atop the cauliflower and mix so that all the pieces are coated.

Place the cauliflower in the dehydrator and spread it out to make a single layer. Sprinkle with a little sea salt and set for 115 degrees, Fahrenheit for 12 to 24 hours or until it becomes exactly as crunchy as you like it. I let mine go for 15 to 16 hours, but the time will vary based on your taste preference as well as the ambient humidity.

Store in an airtight container until serving.

15 Cinnamon Apple Chips with Dip

Preparation time: 3 hours and 30 minutes Cooking time: 3 hours
Servings: 2

Ingredients:

1 cup raw cashews

2 apples, thinly sliced1 lemon
1½ cups water, divided

Cinnamon plus more to dust the chips Another medium cored apple quartered1 tablespoon honey or agave
1 teaspoon cinnamon

¼ teaspoon sea saltDirections:
Place the cashews in a bowl of warm water, deep enough to cover

them and let them soak overnight.

Preheat the oven to 200 degrees, Fahrenheit. Line two baking sheets with parchment paper.

Juice the lemon into a large glass bowl and add two cups of the water. Place the sliced apples in the water as you cut them and when done, swish them around and drain.

Spread the apple slices across the baking sheet in a single layer and sprinkle with a little cinnamon. Bake for 90 minutes.

Remove the slices from the oven and flip each of them over. Put them back in the oven and bake for another 90 minutes, or until they are crisp. Remember, they will get crisper as they cool.

While the apple slices are cooking, drain the cashews and put them in a blender, along with the quartered apple, the honey, a teaspoon of cinnamon and a half cup of the remaining water. Process until thick and creamy. I like to refrigerate my dip for about an hour to chill, before serve alongside the room temperature apple slices.

Smoothies and Beverages

16 Soothing Ginger Tea Drink

Preparation time: 2 hours and 15 minutes Cooking time: 2 hours and 10 minutes Servings: 8
Ingredients:

1 tablespoon of minced ginger root 2 tablespoons of honey
15 green tea bags

32 fluid ounce of white grape juice 2 quarts of boiling water Directions:
Pour water into a 4-quarts slow cooker, immerse tea bags, cover the cooker and let stand for 10 minutes.

After 10 minutes, remove and discard tea bags and stir in remaining ingredients.

Return cover to slow cooker, then plug in and let cook at high heat setting for 2 hours or until heated through.

When done, strain the liquid and serve hot or cold.

Nutrition: Calories:45 Cal, Carbohydrates:12g, Protein:0g, Fats:0g,Fiber:0g.

17 Nice Spiced Cherry Cider

Preparation time: 4 hours and 5 minutes Cooking time: 4 hours

Servings: 16

Ingredients:

2 cinnamon sticks, each about 3 inches long 6-ounce of cherry gelatin

4 quarts of apple cider

Directions:

Using a 6-quarts slow cooker, pour the apple cider and add the cinnamon stick.

Stir, then cover the slow cooker with its lid. Plug in the cooker and let it cook for 3 hours at the high heat setting or until it is heated thoroughly.

Then add and stir the gelatin properly, then continue cooking for another hour.

When done, remove the cinnamon sticks and serve the drink hot or cold.

Nutrition: , Calories:100 Cal, Carbohydrates:0g, Protein:0g, Fats:0g, Fiber:0g.

18 Fragrant Spiced Coffee

Preparation time: 3 hours and 10 minutes Cooking time: 3 hours
Servings: 8

Ingredients:

4 cinnamon sticks, each about 3 inches long 1 1/2 teaspoons of whole cloves
1/3 cup of honey

1-ounce of chocolate syrup 1/2 teaspoon of anise extract 8 cups of brewed coffee Directions:

Pour the coffee in a 4-quarts slow cooker and pour in the remaining ingredients except for cinnamon and stir properly.

Wrap the whole cloves in cheesecloth and tie its corners with strings.

Immerse this cheesecloth bag in the liquid present in the slow cooker and cover it with the lid.

Then plug in the slow cooker and let it cook on the low heat setting for 3 hours or until heated thoroughly.

When done, discard the cheesecloth bag and serve.

Nutrition: Calories:150 Cal, Carbohydrates:35g, Protein:3g, Fats:0g,Fiber:0g.

19 Maca Almond Smoothie

Preparation: 5 min.Cooking: 5 min.Servings: 2

Ingredients:

½ t. vanilla extract

1 scoop maca powder1 tbsp. almond butter

1 c. almond milk, unsweetened2 avocados
Directions:

In a high-speed blender, add all the ingredients and blend untilsmooth. Serve immediately and enjoy!

Nutrition: Calories: 758 | Carbohydrates: 28.6 g | Proteins: 9.3 g |Fats: 72.3 g

20 Blueberry Smoothie

Preparation Time: 5 min.

Cooking Time: 5 min.Serving: 1 Ingredients:
¼ c. pumpkin seeds shelled unsalted 3 c. blueberries, frozen avocados, peeled and halved1 c. almond milk
Directions:

In a high-speed blender, add all the ingredients and blend until smooth.Add two to four ice cubes and blend until smooth.Serve immediately and enjoy!

Nutrition: Calories: 401 | Carbohydrates: 6.3 g | Proteins: 5 g | Fats:

40.3 g

21 Nutty Protein Shake

Preparation Time: 5 min.Cooking Time: 5 min.

Serving: 1 Ingredients:

¼ avocado

2 tbsp. powdered peanut butter1 tbsp. of the following:

- Cocoa powder

- Peanut butter

1 scoop protein powder

½ c. almond milkDirections:

In a high-speed blender, add all the ingredients and blend until

smooth.

Add two to four ice cubes and blend again. Serve immediately and enjoy!

Nutrition: Calories: 694 | Carbohydrates: 30.8 g | Proteins: 40.8 g |Fats: 52 g

22 Cinnamon Pear Smoothie

Preparation: 2 min.Cooking: 2 min.Serving: 1 Ingredients:
1 t. cinnamon scoop vanilla protein powder

½ c. of the following: Almond milk, unsweetenedCoconut Milk

1 pears, cores removed Sweetener of your choice Directions:

In a high-speed blender, add all the ingredients and blend. Add two or more ice cubes and blend again.
Serve immediately and enjoy!

Nutrition: Calories: 653 | Carbohydrates: 75.2 g | Proteins: 28.4 g |Fats: 32.2 g

Snacks and Desserts

23 Plant Based Crispy Falafel

Preparation time: 20 minsCooking time: 30 mins Servings: 8

Ingredients

1 tbsp. extra-virgin olive oil

1 cup dried chickpeas soaked for 24 hours in the refrigerator1 cup cauliflower, chopped
½ cup red onion, chopped

½ cup packed fresh parsley2 cloves garlic, quartered
1 tsp. sea salt

½ tsp. ground black pepper

½ tsp. ground cumin

¼ tsp. ground cinnamonDirections
Preheat oven to 375° F.

In a food processor, mix chickpeas, cauliflower, onion, parsley, garlic, salt, pepper, cumin seeds, cinnamon, and olive oil until mixture is smooth.

Take 2 tbsps. of mixture and make the falafel into small patties.Keep falafel on greased baking tray.

Bake falafel for about 25 to 30 minutes in preheated oven untilgolden brown from both sides.

Once cooked remove from oven.

Serve hot fresh vegetable salad and enjoy!

Nutrition: Protein: 16% 19 kcal Fat: 24% 29 kcal Carbohydrates:

60% 71 kcal

24 Waffles With Almond Flour

Preparation time: 15 minsCooking time: 15 mins Servings: 4

Ingredients

1 cup almond milk 2 tbsps. chia seeds2 tsp lemon juice
4 tbsps. coconut oil 1/2 cup almond flour2 tbsps. maple syrup

Cooking spray or cooking oilDirections

Mix coconut milk with lemon juice in a mixing bowl.

Leave it for 5-8 minutes on room temperature to turn it into buttermilk.

Once coconut milk is turned into butter milk, add chai seeds into milkand whisk together.

Add other ingredients in milk mixture and mix well. Preheat a waffle iron and spray it with coconut oil spray.

Pour 2 tbsp. of waffle mixture into the waffle machine and cook untilgolden.

Top with some berries and serve hot.

Enjoy with black coffee!

Nutrition: Protein: 5% 15 kcal Fat: 71% 199 kcal Carbohydrates:

23% 66 kcal

25 Mint & Avocado Smoothie

Preparation time: 10 mins Cooking time: 0 minutes
Servings: 2
Ingredients

1 cup coconut water1/2 lemon juice
½ cup cucumber

1 cup mint. fresh

1/2 medium size avocadoI/2 tsp maple syrup
1 cup ice

Directions

Place all ingredients into a blender, cover lid and blend until smooth. Blend on high speed until smoothie has fluffy texture.
Pour smoothie in glass and top with mint leaves.

Serve and enjoy!

Nutrition: Protein: 6% 7 kcal Fat: 51% 64 kcal Carbohydrates: 44%

55 kcal

26 Crispy Honey Pecans (Slow Cooker)

Preparation time: 2 hours and 15 minutes Cooking time: 3 hours
Servings: 4

Ingredients

16 oz pecan halves

4 Tbsp coconut butter melted 4 to 5 Tbsp honey strained
1/4 tsp ground ginger
1/4 tsp ground allspice

1 1/2 tsp ground cinnamon Directions
Add pecans and melted coconut butter into your 4-quart SlowCooker.

Stir until combined well. Add in honey and stir well.
In a bowl, combine spices and sprinkle over nuts; stir lightly.

Cook on LOW uncovered for about 2 to 3 hours or until nuts arecrispy.

Serve cold.

27 **Crunchy Fried Pickles**

Preparation time: 10 minutes Cooking time: 5 minutes Servings: 6
Ingredients

1/2 cup Vegetable oil for frying1 cup all-purpose flour
1 cup plain breadcrumbs

Pinch of salt and pepper

30 pickle chips (cucumber, dill)Directions:
Heat oil in a large frying skillet over medium-high heat.

Stir the flour, breadcrumbs, and the salt and pepper in a shallowbowl.

Dredgethe picklesinthelour/breadcrumbsmixturetocoat completely.

Fry in batches until golden brown on all sides, 2 to 3 minutes in total.Drain on paper towels and serve.

28 Granola bars with Maple Syrup

Preparation time: 15 minutes Cooking time: 0 minutes Servings: 12

Ingredients

3/4 cup dates chopped

2 Tbsp chia seeds soaked3/4 cup rolled oats

4 Tbsp Chopped nuts such Macadamia, almond, Brazilian...etc,2 Tbsp shredded coconut

2 Tbsp pumpkin seeds2 Tbsp sesame seeds 2 Tbsp hemp seeds

1/2 cup maple syrup (or to taste) 1/4 cup peanut butter

Directions:

Add all ingredients (except maple syrup and peanut butter) into a food processor and pulse just until roughly combined.

Add maple syrup and peanut butter and process until all ingredientsare combined well.

Place baking paper onto a medium baking dish and spread themixture.

Cover with a plastic wrap and press down to make it flat.

Chill granola in the fridge for one hour.Cut it into 12 bars and serve.

Keep stored in an airtight container for up to 1 week.

Also, you can wrap them individually in parchment paper, and keepin the freezer in a large Ziploc bag.

29 Lemon & Ginger Kale Chips

Preparation Time: 30 Minutes Cooking Time: 10 Minutes
Servings: 5
Ingredients:

Ginger (1 t.) Salt (to Taste)
Lemon Zest (1 t.) Olive Oil (1 T.) Kale (7 Oz.) Directions:
Before you begin cooking this delicious snack, you'll want
to prepare the oven to 300. As this warms up, go ahead
and line your baking sheet with parchment paper.

Next, you are going to want to place your kale into a bowl
and toss with the olive oil, lemon zest, ginger, and the salt.
Give everything a good toss to spread the seasonings over
all of the kale.

When the kale is set, spread it out evenly onto your
baking sheet and pop into the oven for ten minutes. By
the end of this time, the edges of the leaves should look
dry.

If the kale is cooked to your liking, remove from the
oven and allow to cool completely before serving.

Nutrition: Calories: 45 Proteins: 1g Carbs: 4g Fats: 3g

30 Pumpkin Spice Granola Bites

Preparation Time: 2 Hours Cooking Time: 0 Minutes
Servings:
Ingredients:

Pumpkin Pie Spice (.50 t.)

Old-fashioned Rolled Oats (.75 C.)Medjool Dates (15)
Pumpkin Puree (.33 C.)Granola (.50 C.) Directions:
To start off, go ahead and place the oats into a food processor and process until it becomes flour. Once this is done, you will want to add in the spice, pumpkin, and dates. Puree everything again until you get a dough.

From this dough, use your hands to take small bits and roll into ten balls.

Place the balls into the fridge for two hours and allow to firm up.Finally, roll the balls in your favorite granola and then enjoy.
Nutrition: Calories: 100 Proteins: 10g Carbs: 25g Fats: 10g

31 Salted Carrot Fries

Preparation Time: 30 MinutesCooking Time: 20 Minutes

Servings: 4Ingredients:

Olive Oil (2 T.)

Salt (to taste)Carrots (6) Directions:

Begin by prepping your oven to 425. While this warms up, line abaking sheet with parchment paper and set to the side.

Next, you will want to take your carrots and carefully cut them intosmaller sections, resembling fries.

Once the carrots are cut, you will want to toss them in a bowl with the salt and olive oil. As you do this, make sure the carrots areevenly coated.

Finally, pop the dish into the oven for twenty minutes. By the end, thecarrots should be slightly browned and cooked through. If it is cooked to your liking, allow to cool and then enjoy.

Nutrition: Calories: 100 Proteins: 1g Carbs: 11g Fats: 7g

Dinner Recipes

32 Spicy Grilled Tofu Steak

Preparation Time: 30 min.Cooking Time: 20 min.
Servings: 4Ingredients:

1 tbsp. of the following:chopped scallion chopped cilantro soy sauce

hoisin sauce2 tbsp. oil
¼ t. of the following:

salt

garlic powder

red chili pepper powder

ground Sichuan peppercorn powder

½ t. cumin

1 pound firm tofuDirections:

Place the tofu on a plate and drain the excess liquid for about 10 minutes.

Slice drained tofu into ¾ thick stakes.

Stir the cumin, Sichuan peppercorn, chili powder, garlic powder, and salt in a mixing bowl until well-incorporated.

In another little bowl, combine soy sauce, hoisin, and 1 teaspoon of oil.

Heat a skillet to medium temperature with oil, then carefully place thetofu in the skillet.

Sprinkle the spices over the tofu, distributing equally across all steaks. Cook for 3-5 minutes, flip, and put spice on the other side. Cook for an additional 3 minutes.

Brush with sauce and plate.

Sprinkle some scallion and cilantro and enjoy.

Nutrition: Calories: 155 | Carbohydrates: 7.6 g | Proteins: 9.9 g | Fats: 11.8g

33 Stuffed peppers

Preparation time 40 minutes Cooking time: 15 minutes Servings: 8
Ingredients:

2 cans (15 ounces each) black beans, drained, rinsed 2 cups tofu, pressed, crumbled
3/4 cup green onion s, thinly sliced

1/2 cup fresh cilantro, chopped1/4 cup vegetable oil
1/4 cup lime juice

3 cloves garlic, finely chopped1/2 teaspoon salt
1/2 teaspoon chili powder

8 large bell peppers, halved lengthwise, deseeded 3 roma tomatoes, diced
Direction:

Mix together in a bowl all the ingredients except the bell peppers tomake the filling.

Fill the peppers with this mixture.

Cut 8 aluminum foils of size 18 x 12 inches. Place 2 halves on each aluminum foil. Seal the peppers such that there is a gap on thesides.

Grill under direct heat for about 15 minutes.

Sprinkle with some cilantro and serve.

Lunch Recipes

34 Red Lentil And Quinoa Fritters

Preparation Time: 20 minutes Cooking Time: 25 minutes
Serving: 10
Ingredients:

For the Fritters:

1/4 cup (59 grams) chickpea flour 1 ½ cups (354 grams) quinoa
1/4 cup (59 grams) cornmeal 1/2 cup (118 grams) red lentils 2 teaspoons ground turmeric 1/8 teaspoon black bell pepper1/2 teaspoon salt
1/4 cup (59 grams) chopped parsley1 teaspoon cumin
1/4 teaspoon ground cinnamon

1/2 of a lemon, juiced

1 tablespoon Dijon mustard1/4 cup (59 grams) tahini
4 cups (946 ml) vegetable broth

For the Sauce:

1 teaspoon minced garlic1/4 teaspoon salt
1 tablespoon chopped dill

3 tablespoons tahini

1 lemon, juiced

1 cup coconut yogurt, unsweetenedDirections:
Switch on the oven, set it to 400° F and let it preheat.

Take a medium pot, place it over medium-high heat, add lentils and quinoa, pour in vegetable broth, and bring it to a boil.

Switch heat to medium-low level and simmer the grains for 15 minutes until cooked, covering the pot.

When done, let grains cool for 10 minutes, fluff them with a fork and transfer into a large bowl.

Add remaining ingredients for the fritters in it and stir well untilincorporated.

Shape the mixture into ten patties, arrange them on a baking sheet lined with aluminum foil and bake for 25 minutes until golden brown on both sides and thoroughly cooked, turning halfway.

Meanwhile, prepare the yogurt sauce: take a medium bowl, place all the ingredients for it inside and whisk until combined.

Serve fritters with yogurt sauce.

Nutrition: 173 Cal; 4 g Fat; 1 g Saturated Fat; 27 g Carbs; 2 g Fiber;

7 g Protein; 3 g Sugar;

35 Brussels Sprouts & Cranberries Salad

Preparation Time: 10 minutes Cooking Time: 0 minute
Servings: 6
Ingredients:

1 tablespoons lemon juice

¼ cup olive oil

Salt and pepper to taste

1 lb. Brussels sprouts, sliced thinly

¼ cup dried cranberries, chopped

½ cup pecans, toasted and chopped

½ cup vegan parmesan cheese, shavedDirection
Mix the lemon juice, olive oil, salt and pepper in a bowl.

Toss the Brussels sprouts, cranberries and pecans in this mixture.Sprinkle the Parmesan cheese on top.
Nutrition: Calories 245 Total Fat 18.9 g Saturated Fat 9 g Cholesterol3 mg Sodium 350 mg Total Carbohydrate 15.9 g Dietary Fiber 5 g Protein 6.4 g Total Sugars 10 g Potassium 20 mg

36 **Potato Latke**

Preparation Time: 15 minutes Cooking Time: 10 minutes
Servings: 6
Ingredients:

3 eggs, beaten

1 onion, grated

1 ½ teaspoons baking powderSalt and pepper to taste
2 lb. potatoes, peeled and grated

¼ cup all-purpose flour

4 tablespoons vegetable oil Chopped onion chives
Direction
Preheat your oven to 400 degrees F.

In a bowl, beat the eggs, onion, baking powder, salt and pepper. Squeeze moisture from the shredded potatoes using paper towel.Add potatoes to the egg mixture.
Stir in the flour.

Pour the oil into a pan over medium heat.

Cook a small amount of the batter for 3 to 4 minutes per side.Repeat until the rest of the batter is used.
Garnish with the chives.

Nutrition: Calories: 266 Total fat: 11.6g Saturated fat: 2g Cholesterol: 93mg Sodium: 360mg Potassium: 752mg Carbohydrates: 34.6gFiber: 9g Sugar: 3g Protein: 7.5g

37 Rice Bowl with Edamame

Preparation Time: 10 minutes

Cooking Time: 3 hours and 50 minutesServings: 6
Ingredients:

1 tablespoon coconut oil, melted

¾ cup brown rice (uncooked) 1 cup wild rice (uncooked)
Cooking spray
4 cups vegetable stock 8 oz. shelled edamame 1 onion,
chopped
Salt to taste

½ cup dried cherries, sliced

½ cup pecans, toasted and sliced 1 tablespoon red wine
vinegar Direction
Add the rice and coconut oil in a slow cooker sprayed
with oil. Pour in the stock and stir in the edamame and
onions.
Season with salt.

Seal the pot.

Cook on high for 3 hours and 30 minutes.
Stir in the dried cherries.Let sit for 5 minutes.
Stir in the rest of the ingredients before serving.

Nutrition: Calories: 381 Total fat: 12g 18 % Saturated fat:
2g Sodium:459mg Carbohydrates: 61g Fiber: 7g Sugar: 13g

Protein: 12g

38 Spicy Southwestern Hummus Wraps

Preparation: 15 MinutesCooking: 0 Minutes Servings: 1
Ingredients:

Whole-wheat Wrap (1) Lettuce (1 C., Shredded)Tomato (1 T., Diced) Hummus (4 T.) Avocado (2 T., Diced)Corn (2 T.) Black Beans (2 T.)Directions:

For a quick lunch, simply lay out your wrap and spread the hummus

over the surface.

Once the hummus is in place, layer the rest of the ingredients andthen roll the wrap up before eating.

Nutrition: Calories: 400 Proteins: 15g Carbs: 50g Fats: 15g

39 Buffalo Cauliflower Wings

Preparation Time: 30 Minutes Cooking Time: 15 Minutes
Servings: 4
Ingredients:

Chickpea Flour (.75 C) Almond Milk (1 C.) Buffalo Sauce (1 C.)

Cauliflower (1 Head) Curry Powder (1 t.) Onion Powder (1 t.) Garlic Powder (1 t.) Nutritional Yeast (2 T.)
Directions:

You will want to begin this recipe by prepping the oven to 450. As this warms up, go ahead and prep a baking sheet with parchment paper and then set it to the side.

Next, you are going to take a bowl and combine the nutritional yeast and spices with the flour.

With your flour made up, carefully dip the cauliflower into the soymilk and directly into the flour. Once the cauliflower piece is well coated, place it onto your baking sheet and continue until you have covered every cauliflower floret.

When you are ready, pop the baking dish into the oven for about twenty minutes. After this time, the cauliflower should be crispy.

Once the cauliflower is cooked through, place it into a bowl, and toss with the hot sauce. When all of the pieces are well coated, place them back into the oven for another ten minutes, and then they will be ready.

Nutrition: Calories: 160 Proteins: 11g Carbs: 20g Fats: 3g

40 Veggie Fritters

Preparation: 35 MinutesCooking: 20 Minutes Servings: 4

Ingredients:

Flour (2 C.) Cabbage (4 C., Cut) Carrots (2 C., Sliced) Shallots (3) Water (1.25 C.)

Garlic Cloves (3)Olive Oil (2 T.) Salt (to Taste) Powdered Mushroom Stock (15 t.)Pepper (to Taste) Directions:

You will want to begin this recipe by crushing the pepper, salt, mushroom powder, garlic, and shallots together. By the end, you should have created a paste.

In another bowl, go ahead and mix together the paste, water, carrot slices, cabbage., and the flour together. From this, you will be creating a thick, chunky batter.

Now that your batter is made, you'll want to begin to heat a pan over medium heat and then place the oil in once warm.As the oil begins to sizzle, create 1-inch patties with your batter and lay them in the pan like pancakes. After frying the patty for five minutes on one side, flip it over and cook the other side until both sides reach a nice golden color.

Once you are done cooking, pat the fritter down with a paper towel toremove excess oil, and then you can enjoy!

Nutrition: Calories: 330 Proteins: 10g Carbs: 60g Fats: 6g

41 Tomato, Green Beans and Chard Soup

Preparation time: 10 minutes Cooking time: 35 minutes Servings: 4
Ingredients:

2 scallions, chopped

1 cup swiss chard, chopped1 tablespoon olive oil
1 red bell pepper, chopped

Salt and black pepper to the taste1 cup tomatoes, cubed
1 cup green beans, chopped6 cups vegetable stock
2 tablespoons tomato passata

2 garlic cloves, minced

2 teaspoons thyme, chopped

½ Teaspoon red pepper flakesDirections:
Heat up a pot with the oil over medium heat, add the scallions, garlic and the pepper flakes and sauté for 5 minutes.

Add the chard and the other ingredients, toss, bring to a simmer andcook over medium heat for 30 minutes more.

Ladle the soup into bowls and serve for lunch. Nutrition: calories 150, fat 8, fiber 2, carbs 4, protein 9

Recipes For Main Courses And Single Dishes

42 Thai Seitan Vegetable Curry

Preparation Time: 20 minutes Cooking Time: 15 minutes
Servings: 4
Ingredients:

1 tbsp vegetable oil4 cups diced seitan
1 cup sliced mixed bell peppers

½ cup onions diced

1 small head broccoli, cut into florets2 tbsp Thai red curry paste
1 tsp garlic puree

1 cup unsweetened coconut milk2 tbsp vegetable broth
2 cups spinach

Salt and black pepper to tasteDirections:

Heat the vegetable oil in a large skillet over medium heat and fry the

seitan until slightly dark brown. Mix in the bell peppers, onions,broccoli, and cook until softened, 4 minutes.

Mix the curry paste, garlic puree, and 1 tablespoon of coconut milk. Cook for 1 minute and stir in the remaining coconut milk and vegetable broth. Simmer for 10 minutes.

Stir in the spinach to wilt and season the curry with salt and blackpepper.

Serve the curry with steamed white or brown rice.

43 Tofu Cabbage Stir-Fry

Preparation Time: 15 minutes Cooking Time: 10 minutes
Servings: 4
Ingredients:

5 oz. vegan butter

2 ½ cups baby bok choy, quartered lengthwise 8 oz sliced mushrooms
2 cups extra-firm tofu, pressed and cubed Salt and black pepper to taste
1 tsp onion powder 1 tsp garlic powder 1 tbsp plain vinegar
2 garlic cloves, minced 1 tsp chili flakes
1 tbsp fresh ginger, grated

3 scallions, sliced 1 tbsp sesame oil
1 cup vegan mayonnaise Wasabi paste to taste
Cooked white or brown rice (1/2 cup per person)
Directions:

Melt half of the vegan butter in a wok and sauté the bok choy until softened, 3 minutes.

Season with salt, black pepper, onion powder, garlic powder, and vinegar. Sauté for 2 minutes to combine the flavors and plate the bokchoy.

Melt the remaining vegan butter in the wok and sauté the garlic, mushrooms, chili flakes, and ginger until fragrant.

Stir in the tofu and cook until browned on all sides. Add

the scallions and bok choy, heat for 2 minutes and drizzle in the sesame oil.

In a small bowl, mix the vegan mayonnaise and wasabi, and mix into the tofu and vegetables. Cook for 2 minutes and dish the food.

Serve warm with steamed rice.

44 Curried Tofu with Buttery Cabbage

Preparation Time: 15 minutes Cooking Time: 10 minutes
Servings: 4
Ingredients:

2 cups extra-firm tofu, pressed and cubed 1 tbsp + 3 ½ tbsp coconut oil
½ cup unsweetened shredded coconut

1 tsp yellow curry powder1 tsp salt
½ tsp onion powder

2 cups Napa cabbage4 oz. vegan butter
Salt and black pepper to taste

Lemon wedges for servingDirections:

In a medium bowl, add the tofu, 1 tablespoon of coconut oil, curry powder, salt, and onion powder. Mix well until the tofu is well-coated with the spices.

Heat the remaining coconut oil in a non-stick skillet and fry the tofu until golden brown on all sides, 8 minutes. Divide onto serving platesand set aside for serving.

In another skillet, melt half of the vegan butter, and sauté the cabbage until slightly caramelized, 2 minutes. Season with salt, black pepper, and plate to the side of the tofu.

Melt the remaining vegan butter in the skillet and drizzle all over the cabbage.

Serve warm.

Nutrient-Packed Protein Salads

45 Black Bean Lentil Salad With Lime Dressing

Preparation time: 5 mins.Cooking time: 0 mins.

Ingredient: 1 cup green/brown lentils (uncooked)

15 oz. can black beans1 red bell pepper

1/2 small red onion 1-2 roma tomatoes

2/3 cup cilantro (stems removed) Optional: green onion.

Juice of 1 lime

2 Tbsp. olive oil (omit for oil-free)1 tsp. Dijon mustard

1-2 cloves garlic (minced)

1 tsp. cumin

1/2 tsp. oregano1/8 tsp. salt

Optional: chipotle powder, chili powder, pepper, hot sauce, otherseasonings, etc.

Directions:

Cook lentils according to package directions, leaving firm not mushy.Drain.

While lentils are cooking, make the dressing: place all ingredients in a small bowl and whisk to combine. Set aside. Finely dice the bell pepper, onion, and tomatoes. Roughly chop the cilantro. In a large bowl, place the black beans (rinsed and drained), bell pepper, onion, tomatoes, and lentils. Add the dressing and toss to combine. Add cilantro, and lightly toss. Serve immediately or chill covered in the fridge for at least an hour to let the flavors combine.

Flavour Boosters (Fish Glazes, Meat Rubs & Fish Rubs)

46 Teriyaki Tangy Fish Glaze

Rice wine paired with tangy orange juice make it a perfect fish meal to have on any given day. This saucy Teriyaki glaze brings out the juicy, mild flavors of fish. Try out this on weekend and impressyourself!

Preparation Time: 5 min.Cooking Time: 5 min.
Servings: 1 ¼ cup/10 oz.Ingredients:
Rice wine - 1/4 cup

Orange juice, with pulp - 3/4 cupSoy sauce - 3 tbs.
Minced scallions - 1 tbs.Honey - 1 tbs.
Orange slices – for garnishingLemon juice - 1 tsp.
Directions:

To make the teriyaki glaze, combine the mentioned fish marinade ingredients in your food processor or blender. Gently blend the ingredients.

Now, take your favorite cooked/grilled/baked baked salmon or any other fish variety. Gently spread or pour the prepared glaze over the cuts. Allow a few minutes for the glaze to set in. Enjoy the teriyaki glazed fish meal!

47 Extra Scrumptious Super Meat & Fish Rubs

Spice up your dream meats and fish with some extra flavors of the following handpicked collection of meat as well as fish rubs to put anend to your spicy food cravings.

Rubs – How Much is Adequate for your Meat?

•   For meat cuts including steak, chicken, and pork, using rubmixture of 1 tbs. (3 tsp.) per 16 oz. piece is suggested.

•   For variety of fish, rub mixture of ½ tbs. (1 to 2 tsp.) to 1 tbs. (3tsp.) per 16 oz. piece is adequate.

•   To be safe, use less quantity for the first time to determine itsspice strength. You will be able to adjust the quantity next time.

48 Long Island Spiced Rub

Tickle your taste buds with a vibrant spice mixture of cinnamon, nutmeg, black pepper, and cloves. Fish meals spiced with this rub make perfect combo with your choice of fresh salad along with lime drink or juice; it is also a great choice to pair up with coconut and pineapple salsa.

Preparation Time: 5 min.Cooking Time: 5 min.
Servings: 16-18 tsp.

Ingredients:

Nutmeg - 2 tsp.

All-spice - 1 tbsp.

Cinnamon - 2 tsp. Ground ginger - 2 tsp.Garlic powder - 2 tsp.

Ground black pepper - 2 tsp.Ground cloves - 1 tsp.
Cayenne pepper - 2 tsp.

Sugar - 1½ tbsp.

Salt - 1½ tbsp.

Directions:

Mix in all mentioned ingredients in your mixing bowl to make the longisland rub. Gently mix all ingredients using spatula or spoon to form an aromatic rub mixture.

Now, take your choice of fish and place it on a firm surface. Brush or rub the freshly made rub on it; pat gently for the rub onto stick on the surface. Turn it and repeat to spice up its other side.

Let your fish cuts adequately season for more rich flavors for some time in your refrigerator.

*Do not let your fish season for more than 2 hours (but not less than 30 minutes).

Take it out, as it is ready to be cooked or grilled!

Sauce Recipes

49 Vegan High-Protein Queso

Preparation time: 5 minutesCooking time: 5 minutes

Servings: 2Ingredients:

1/4 cup nutritional yeast

1/2 block tofu

3 tablespoon lemon juice 1/4 teaspoon tapioca starch1/4 teaspoon garlic powder 1/4 teaspoon turmeric

1/4 teaspoon onion powder1/4 cup water

1/2 teaspoon saltDirections:

Add tofu, yeast, starch, lemon juice, salt, garlic powder, turmeric and

onion powder and blend until well mixed.

Add water as desired. Heat in a microwave for 30 seconds. Serve and enjoy.

50 Vegan Buffalo Sauce

Preparation time: 5 minutes Cooking time: 5 minutes Servings: 1 cup Ingredients:

1/2 cup soy milk1 cup hot sauce1/2 cup vinegar

1/2 teaspoon pepper2 tablespoons sugar

1/2 teaspoon garlic granules

1 tablespoon tomato sauceDirections:

Mix soy milk, hot sauce, sugar, vinegar, sugar, pepper, tomato sauce

and garlic granules in a pan and cook over medium heat for 10minutes.

Let cool and serve.

Plant Based Diet Cookbook for Beginners with Pictures

Tasty and Quick Recipes to Purify and Energize Your Body

Frank Smith

Breakfasts

1. Vegetable Rice

Preparation time: 7 minutes Cooking time: 15 minutes
Servings: 4
Ingredients:

½ cup brown rice, rinsed1 cup water
½ teaspoon dried basil

1 small onion, chopped2 tablespoons raisins
5 ounces frozen peas, thawed

½ cup pecan halves, toasted

1 medium carrot, cut into matchsticks4 green onions, cut
into 1-inch pieces1 tablespoon olive oil
½ teaspoon salt or to taste

½ teaspoon crushed red chili flakes or to taste Ground
pepper or to taste

Directions:

Place a small saucepan with water over medium heat. When it begins to boil, add rice and basil. Stir.
When it again begins to boil, lower the heat and cover with a lid.

Cook for 15 minutes until all the water is absorbed and rice is

cooked. Add more water if you think the rice is not cooked well. Meanwhile, place a skillet over medium high heat. Add carrots, raisins and onions and sauté until the vegetables are crisp as well astender.

Stir in the peas, salt, pepper and chili flakes. Add pecans and rice and stir.
Serve.

Nutrition: Calories 305, Fats 13 g, Carbohydrates 41 g, Proteins 8 g

2. Courgette Risotto

Preparation: 10 minutesCooking: 5 minutes Servings: 8
Ingredients:

2 tablespoons olive oil 4 cloves garlic, finely chopped

1.5 pounds Arborio rice6 tomatoes, chopped
2 teaspoons chopped rosemary

6 courgettes, finely diced

1 ¼ cups peas, fresh or frozen12 cups hot vegetable stock
1 cup chopped

Salt to taste

Freshly ground pepperDirections:
Place a large heavy bottomed pan over medium heat. Add oil. When

the oil is heated, add onion and sauté until translucent.Stir in the tomatoes and cook until soft.
Next stir in the rice and rosemary. Mix well.

Add half the stock and cook until dry. Stir frequently.Add remaining stock and cook for 3-4 minutes.

Add courgette and peas and cook until rice is tender. Add salt andpepper to taste.

Stir in the basil. Let it sit for 5 minutes.

Nutrition: Calories 406, Fats 5 g, Carbohydrates 82 g, Proteins 14 g

3. Country Breakfast Cereal

Preparation Time: 5 minutes Cooking time: 40 minutes Servings: 6

Ingredients:

1 cup brown rice, uncooked

½ cup raisins, seedless1 tsp cinnamon, ground
¼ Tbsp peanut butter2 ¼ cups water Honey, to taste
Nuts, toastedDirections:

Combine rice, butter, raisins, and cinnamon in a saucepan. Add 2 ¼

cups water. Bring to boil.

Simmer covered for 40 minutes until rice is tender. Fluff with fork. Add honey and nuts to taste.

Nutrition: Calories 160 Carbohydrates 34 g Fats 1.5 g Protein 3 g

4. Root Vegetable Hash With Avocado Crème

Preparation time: 25 mCooking time: 10 m Ingredients:
1/2 c onion, diced1 T vegan butter
1 cloves garlic, minced

1 c sweet potatoes, diced1 c turnips, diced
1 c broccoli florets, diced2 vegan sausages, diced
1 c collard greens, chopped

1/2 tsp sea salt1 tsp cumin
1/2 tsp black pepper

1/4 – 1/2c vegetable stock 1/4 c fresh cilantro, chopped1 medium avocado
1 T balsamic vinegar1/4 c cashews Directions:

Melt and hest the butter in a skillet. Add onion and garlic and sautéuntil they are translucent about 5 minutes.

Add sweet potatoes and turnips stir to match. Cook for 5-8 minutes.

Add the broccoli and vegetables. Continue cooking until it turns light green and start to soften for 5 to 8 minutes.

Add the roasted field, salt, pepper, cumin, coriander, and vinegar. Reduce the heat and get it cooked until the meat is hot and the flavors melt.

Mix the avocado, cashews, and vegetable broth in a blender until smooth.

Plate and serve with a spoonful of avocado cream on top. Garnish with more cilantro.

Nutrition: 19 g fat 30 g of carbohydrates 17 g protein 7 g sugar 691 mg sodium

5. Warm Maple and Cinnamon Quinoa

Preparation time: 5 minutes Cooking time: 15 minutes Servings: 4

Ingredients

1 cup unsweetened nondairy milk1 cup water
1 cup quinoa, rinsed

1 teaspoon cinnamon

¼ Cup chopped pecans or other nuts or seeds, such as chia,sunflower seeds, or almonds

2 tablespoons pure maple syrup or agaveDirections:

In a medium saucepan over medium-high heat, bring the almond milk, water, and quinoa to a boil. Lower the heat to medium-low and cover. Simmer until the liquid is mostly absorbed and the quinoa softens, about 15 minutes.

Turn off the heat and allow to sit, covered, for 5 minutes. Stir in the cinnamon, pecans, and syrup. Serve hot.

6. Warm Quinoa Breakfast Bowl

Preparation time: 5 minutes Cooking time: 0 minutes Servings: 4
Ingredients

3 cups freshly cooked quinoa

1 ⅓ cups unsweetened soy or almond milk 2 bananas, sliced

1 cup raspberries

1 cup blueberries

½ Cup chopped raw walnuts

¼ Cup maple syrupDirections:
Divide the Ingredients among 4 bowls, starting with a base of ¾ cup

quinoa,⅓cupmilk,½banana,¼cupraspberries,¼ cup blueberries, and 2 tablespoons walnuts.

Drizzle 1 tablespoon of maple syrup over the top of each bowl.

7. Banana Bread Rice Pudding

Preparation time: 5 minutes Cooking time: 50 minutes Servings: 4

Ingredients 1cup brown rice1½ cups water

1½ cups nondairy milk

3 tablespoons sugar (omit if using a sweetened nondairy milk)2 teaspoons pumpkin pie spice or ground cinnamon

2 bananas

3 tablespoons chopped walnuts or sunflower seeds (optional)Directions

In a medium pot, combine the rice, water, milk, sugar, and pumpkin

pie spice. Bring to a boil over high heat, turn the heat to low, and cover the pot. Simmer, stirring occasionally, until the rice is soft and the liquid is absorbed. White rice takes about 20 minutes; brown rice takes about 50 minutes.

Smash the bananas and stir them into the cooked rice. Serve topped with walnuts (if using). Leftovers will keep refrigerated in an airtight container for up to 5 days.

Nutrition: calories: 479; protein: 9g; total fat: 13g; saturated fat: 1g; carbohydrates: 86g; fiber: 7g

8. Breakfast Smoothie

Preparation: 10 minutesCooking: 0 minute Servings: 2
Ingredients:

½ cup strawberries ½ cup mango, sliced

½ banana, sliced ½ cup coconut milk

1 tablespoon cashew butter 1 tablespoon ground chia seeds Directions: ut all the ingredients in a blender. Pulse until smooth. Refrigerate overnight.

Nutrition: Calories: 299 Total fat: 14.5g Saturated fat: 4.2g Sodium: 64mg Potassium: 599mg Carbohydrates: 42.4g Fiber: 8.5g Sugar: 23g Protein: 5.3g

9. Yogurt with Beets & Raspberries

Preparation: 5 minutesCooking 0 minute Servings: 1
Ingredients:

1 cup soy yogurt

½ cup beets, cooked and sliced1 tablespoon raspberry jam
1 tablespoon almonds, sliveredDirections:
Mix all the ingredients in a glass jar with lid. Sprinkle the almonds on top.
Refrigerate for up to 2 days.

Nutrition: Calories: 281 Total fat: 7.3g Saturated fat: 2.7g Cholesterol: 15mg Sodium: 237mg Potassium: 882mg Carbohydrates: 40.2g Fiber: 2.5g Sugar: 36g

10. **Curry Oatmeal**

Preparation Time: 10 minutes Cooking Time: 0 minute
Servings: 3
Ingredients:

1 tablespoon pure peanut butter

½ cup rolled oats

½ cup coconut milk

½ teaspoon curry powder1 teaspoon tamari
¼ cup cooked kale

1 tablespoon cilantro, chopped

2 tablespoons tomatoes, choppedDirections:
Mix all the ingredients except the kale, cilantro and tomatoes.Transfer to a glass jar with lid.
Refrigerate for up to 5 days.

Top with the remaining ingredients when ready to serve.

Nutrition: Calories: 307 Total fat: 13.8g Saturated fat: 4g Cholesterol: 12mg Sodium: 467mg Potassium: 890mg Carbohydrates: 34.1g Fiber: 3g Sugar: 2g Protein: 10.1g

11. Peanut Butter Granola

Preparation time: 10 minutes Cooking time: 47 minutes
Servings: 04
Ingredients:

Nonstick spray4 cups oats

⅓ cup of cocoa powder

¾ cup peanut butter

⅓ cup maple syrup ⅓ cup avocado oil

1½ teaspoons vanilla extract

½ cup cocoa nibs

6 ounces dark chocolate, choppedDirections:
Preheat your oven to 300 degrees F. Spray a baking sheet
with cooking spray.In a medium saucepan add oil, maple
syrup, and peanut butter.

Cook for 2 minutes on medium heat, stirring.Add the oats
and cocoa powder, mix well.
Spread the coated oats on the baking sheet.

Bake for 45 minutes, occasionally stirring.

Garnish with dark chocolate, cocoa nibs, and peanut
butter.Serve.

Nutrition:Calories134TotalFat4.7gSaturatedFat0.6gCholes
terol 124mg Sodium 1 mg Total Carbs 54.1 g Fiber 7 g
ugar

3.3 g Protein 6.2 g

Soups, Salads, and Sides

12. Rainbow Orzo Salad

Preparation time: 10 minutes Cooking time: 20 minutes
Servings: 1
Ingredients:

1 chopped onion

25g grated feta cheese2 sliced bell peppers
1 tablespoon olive oil6 sliced tomatoes
2 tablespoons chopped basil25g orzo pasta
Directions:

Preheat the oven at 350f temperature. Prepare a baking sheet and place the onion and bell peppers and drizzle half olive oil. Bake it for around 15 minutes. Add tomatoes on it and bake for an additional 5 minutes. Meanwhile, cook the orzo according to the given directions on the pack and cool it. Now toss it with the baked vegetables and top it with cheese, basil and remaining oil and serve it.

Nutrition: Carbohydrates 52g, protein 13g, fats 18g, calories 422, sugar 30g.

13. Broccoli Pasta Salad

Preparation time: 15 minutes Chilling time: 30 minutes
Servings: 12
Ingredients:

1-pound cooked pasta 2 diced broccoli florets 1 chopped onion
1 cup grated cheese

12 ounce cooked and finely chopped bacon

¾ teaspoon salt

¾ teaspoon ground black pepper1 cup mayonnaise
Directions:

Take a bowl and mix all the ingredients until all of them combined well. Cover it with the plastic wrap and place it in the refrigerator for at least 30 minutes and serve it. You can keep it in the refrigerator for3 days.

Nutrition: Carbohydrates 36g, protein 14g, fats 29g, calories 461.

14. Eggplant & Roasted Tomato Farro Salad

Preparation time: 1 hour Cooking time: 1 hour 30 minutes Servings: 3

Ingredients:

4 small eggplants

1 ½ cups chopped cherry tomatoes

¾ cup uncooked faro1 tablespoon olive oil1 minced garlic clove
½ cup rinsed and drained chickpeas1 tablespoon basil
1 tablespoon arugula

½ teaspoon salt and ground black pepper 1 tablespoon vinegar
½ cup toasted pine nuts

Directions:

Preheat the oven at 300f temperature and prepare a baking sheet. Place cherry tomatoes on the baking liner and drizzle olive oil, salt, and black pepper on it and bake it for 30 to 35 minutes. Cook thefaro in the salted water for 30 to 40 minutes. Slice the eggplant and salt it and leave it for 30 minutes. After that, rinse it with water and dry it kitchen towel. Now peeled and sliced the eggplants. Now placethese slices on the baking liner and season it with salt, pepper and olive oil. Bake it for 15 to 20 minutes in the preheated oven at the 450f temperature. Flip the sides of eggplant and bake it for an additional 15 to 20 minutes. Bake the pine nuts for 5 minutes and sauté the garlic. Now mix all the ingredients in a bowl and serve it.

Nutrition: Carbohydrates 37g, protein 9g, fats 25g, calories 399.

Entrées

15. Garlicky Kale Chips

Preparation time: 1 hour and 30 minCooking time: 1 hour
Servings: 2

Ingredients:

4 cloves garlic1 cup olive oil
8 to 10 cups fresh kale, chopped

1 tablespoon of garlic-flavored olive oil

½ teaspoon garlic salt

½ teaspoon pepper

1 pinch red pepper flakes (optional)Directions:
Peel and crush the garlic clove and place it in a small jar
with a lid.

Pour the olive oil over the top, cover tightly and shake.

This will keep in the refrigerator for several days. When you're ready to use it, strain out the garlic and retain the oil.

Preheat the oven to 175 degrees, Fahrenheit.

Spread out the kale on a baking sheet and drizzle with the olive oil. Sprinkle with garlic salt, pepper and red pepper flakes.

Bake for an hour, remove from the oven and let the chips cool. Store in an airtight container if you don't plan to eat them right away.

16. Hummus-stuffed Baby Potatoes

Preparation time: 30 minutes Cooking time: 30 minutes
Servings: 2
Ingredients:

12 small red potatoes, walnut-sized or slightly larger
Hummus
2 green onions, thinly sliced

¼ teaspoon paprika, for garnishDirections:
Place two to three inches of water in a saucepan, set a steamerinside and bring the water to a boil.

Place the whole potatoes in the steamer basket and steam for about 20 minutes or until soft. Keep the pan from boiling dry by adding additional hot water as needed.

Dump the potatoes into a colander and run cold water over themuntil they can be handled.

Cut each potato open and scoop out most of the pulp, leaving the skin and a thin layer of potato intact.

Mix the hummus with most of the green onions (keep enough for garnish) and spoon a little into the area where the potato has been scooped out.

Sprinkle each filled potato half with paprika and serve.

Smoothies and Beverages

17. Ultimate Mulled Wine

Preparation: 35 minutesCooking: 30 minutes Servings: 6
Ingredients:

1 cup of cranberries, fresh2 oranges, juiced

1 tablespoon of whole cloves

2 cinnamon sticks, each about 3 inches long1 tablespoon of star anise

1/3 cup of honey 8 fluid ounce of apple cider

8 fluid ounce of cranberry juice24 fluid ounce of red wine
Directions:

Using a 4 quarts slow cooker, add all the ingredients and stirproperly.

Cover it with the lid, then plug in the slow cooker and cook it for 30minutes on thee high heat setting or until it gets warm thoroughly.

When done, strain the wine and serve right away.

Nutrition: Calories:202 Cal, Carbohydrates:25g, Protein:0g, Fats:0g,Fiber:0g.

18. **Pleasant Lemonade**

Preparation time: 3 hours and 15 minutes Cooking time: 3 hours

Servings: 10 servings

Ingredients:

Cinnamon sticks for serving 2 cups of coconut sugar 1/4 cup of honey

3 cups of lemon juice. fresh 32 fluid ounce of water

Directions:

Using a 4-quarts slow cooker, place all the ingredients except for the cinnamon sticks and stir properly.

Cover it with the lid, then plug in the slow cooker and cook it for 3 hours on the low heat setting or until it is heated thoroughly.

When done, stir properly and serve with the cinnamon sticks.

Nutrition: Calories:146 Cal, Carbohydrates:34g, Protein:0g, Fats:0g,Fiber:0g.

19. Pineapple, Banana & Spinach Smoothie

Preparation: 10 MinutesCooking: 0 minute Servings: 1
Ingredients:

½ cup almond milk ¼ cup soy yogurt1 cup spinach
1 cup banana

1 cup pineapple chunks1 tbsp. chia seeds Direction:
Add all the ingredients in a blender.Blend until smooth.
Chill in the refrigerator before serving.

Nutrition: Calories 297, Total Fat 6 g, Saturated Fat 1 g,
Cholesterol4 mg Sodium 145 mg, Total Carbohydrate 54
g, Dietary Fiber 10 g Protein 13g, Total Sugars 29g,
Potassium 1038 mg

20. White Chocolate Pudding

Preparation Time: 4 hours 20 minutes

Servings: 4Ingredients
3 tbsp flax seed + 9 tbsp water 3 tbsp cornstarch ¼ tbsp salt 1 cup cashew cream 2 ½ cups almond milk
½ pure date sugar 1 tbsp vanilla caviar
6 oz unsweetened white chocolate chips Whipped coconut cream for topping
Sliced bananas and raspberries for topping

Directions

In a small bowl, mix the flax seed powder with water and allow thickening for 5 minutes to make the flax egg.

In a large bowl, whisk the cornstarch and salt, and then slowly mix inthe in the cashew cream until smooth. Whisk in the flax egg until wellcombined.

Pour the almond milk into a pot and whisk in the date sugar. Cook over medium heat while frequently stirring until the sugar dissolves. Reduce the heat to low and simmer until steamy and bubbly around the edges.

Pour half of the almond milk mixture into the flax egg mix, whisk well and pour this mixture into the remaining milk content in the pot. Whisk continuously until well combined.

Bring the new mixture to a boil over medium heat while still frequently stirring and scraping all the corners of the pot, 2 minutes.

Turn the heat off, stir in the vanilla caviar, then the white chocolate chips until melted. Spoon the mixture into a bowl, allow cooling for 2 minutes, cover with plastic wraps making sure to press the plastic onto the surface of the pudding, and refrigerate for 4 hours.

Remove the pudding from the fridge, take off the plastic wrap and whip for about a minute.

Spoon the dessert into serving cups, swirl some coconut whipping cream on top, and top with the bananas and raspberries. Enjoyimmediately.

Nutritional info per serving

Calories 654 | Fats 47.9g| Carbs 52.1g | Protein 7.3g

21. Ambrosia Salad With Pecans

Preparation Time: 15 minutes + 1 hour chillingServings: 4
These are the ingredients that inflict anguish if skipped at thecelebration plate.

Ingredients

1 cup pure coconut cream

½ tsp vanilla extract

2 medium bananas, peeled and cut into chunks 1 ½ cups unsweetened coconut flakes
4 tbsp toasted pecans, chopped

1 cup pineapple tidbits, drained

1 (11 oz) can mandarin oranges, drained

¾ cup maraschino cherries, stems removedDirections
In medium bowl, mix the coconut cream and vanilla extract until wellcombined.

In a larger bowl, combine the bananas, coconut flakes, pecans, pineapple, oranges, and cherries until evenly distributed.

Pour on the coconut cream mixture and fold well into the salad. Chill in the refrigerator for 1 hour and serve afterwards.

Nutritional info per serving

Calories 648 | Fats 36g| Carbs 85.7g | Protein 6.6g

22. Peanut Butter Blossom Biscuits

Preparation: 15 minutes + 1 hour chillingServings: 4
Ingredients

1 tbsp flax seed powder + 3 tbsp water

1 cup pure date sugar + more for dusting

½ cup creamy peanut butter1 tsp vanilla extract
1 ¾ cup whole-wheat flour1 tsp baking soda
¼ tsp salt ¼ cup unsweetened chocolate chipsDirections
In a small bowl, mix the flax seed powder with
water and allow

thickening for 5 minutes to make the flax egg.

In a medium bowl using an electric mixer, whisk the date sugar, plantbutter, and peanut butter until light and fluffy.

Mix in the flax egg and vanilla until well combined. Add the flour, baking soda, salt, and whisk well again.

Fold in the chocolate chips, cover the bowl with a plastic wrap, and refrigerate for 1 hour. After, preheat the oven to 375 F and line a baking sheet with parchment paper.

Use a cookie sheet to scoop mounds of the batter onto the sheetwith 1-inch intervals. Bake in the oven for 9 to 10 minutes or until golden brown and slightly cracked on top. Remove the cookies from the oven, cool for 3 minutes, roll in some date sugar, and serve. Nutritional info per serving Calories 839 | Fats 52.5g| Carbs 77.9g | Protein 21.1g

23. Chocolate & Almond Butter Barks

Preparation Time: 35 minutesServings: 4

Chewy fluffy almonds is equal to delicious almond bark, handmade

dairy-free chocolate bars!Ingredients

1/3 cup coconut oil, melted

¼ cup almond butter, melted

2 tbsp unsweetened coconut flakes. 1 tsp pure maple syrup

A pinch ground rock salt

¼ cup unsweetened cocoa nibsDirections

Line a baking tray with baking paper and set aside.

In a medium bowl, mix the coconut oil, almond butter, coconut flakes,maple syrup, and then fold in the rock salt and cocoa nibs.

Pour and spread the mixture on the baking sheet, chill in therefrigerator for 20 minutes or until firm.

Remove the dessert, break into shards and enjoy immediately.Preserve extras in the refrigerator.

Nutritional info per serving

Calories 279 | Fats 28.1g| Carbs 8.6g | Protein 4.4g

Snacks and Desserts

24. Raspberries & Cream Ice Cream

Preparation time: 5 minsCooking time: 0 mins Servings: 4
Ingredients

2 Cups Raspberries 8 Oz. Coconut Cream
2 Tbsps. Coconut Flour

1 Tsp Maple Syrup

4-8 Raspberries For FillingDirections
Mix all ingredients in food processor and blend until well combined.

Spoon mixture into silicone mold and with raspberries and freeze forabout 4 hours.

Remove balls from freezer and pop them out of the molds.Serve immediately and enjoy!
Nutrition: Protein: 5% 12 kcal Fat: 69% 170 kcal

Carbohydrates:

26% 63 kcal

25. **Healthy Chocolate Mousse**

Preparation time: 5 minsCooking time: 0 mins Servings: 2
Ingredients

1/2 Cup Coconut Milk1 Tsp. Maple Syrup
1-3 Tbsps. Cocoa Powder

Pinch Instant Coffee

2 Tbsps. Coconut Cream Blackberries For Topping
Directions
Heat up coconut milk and maple syrup until it just begins
to simmer.Add cocoa and coffee in milk mixture.
Add cream to same mixture and whip until relatively stiff
peaks form.Transfer to a serving glass.
Chill the mousse in freezer for 2-3 hours.

Top with some berries and spoon of coconut cream.
Enjoy!
Nutrition: Protein: 3% 7 kcal Fat: 83% 163 kcal
Carbohydrates: 13%

26 kcal

26. Coconut Rice With Mangos

Preparation time: 15 minsCooking time: 40 mins Servings: 6

Ingredients

2 Cups Coconut Milk

1-1/2 Cups Coconut Flakes1/4 Cup Maple Syrup
1 Mango SlicedDirections
Heat saucepan over high heat.

Add coconut milk and bring it to boil. Stir in coconut flakes and maple syrup.

Cover and cook on low heat for about 15 minutes or until liquid is

completely dried.

Pour coconut rice in plate.

Serve with mango slice and enjoy.

Nutrition: Protein: 3% 8 kcal Fat: 69% 185 kcal Carbohydrates: 28%

75 kcal

27. Honey Peanut Butter

Preparation time: 10 minutes Cooking time: 0 minutes Servings: 6
Ingredients

1 cup peanut butter

3/4 cup honey extracted 1/2 cup ground peanuts 1 tsp ground cinnamon Directions:
Add all ingredients into your fast-speed blender, and blend untilsmooth.

Keep refrigerated.

28. **Mediterranean Marinated Olives**

Preparation time: 10 minutes Cooking time: 0 minutes Servings: 2

Ingredients

24 large olives, black, green, Kalamata1/2 cup extra-virgin olive oil

4 cloves garlic, thinly sliced 2 Tbsp fresh lemon juice

2 tsp coriander seeds, crushed1/2 tsp crushed red pepper

1 tsp dried thyme1 tsp dried rosemary, crushed Salt and ground pepper to taste

Directions:

Place olives and all remaining ingredients in a large container orbag, and shake to combine well.

Cover and refrigerate to marinate overnight.Serve.

Keep refrigerated.

29. **Nut Butter & Dates Granola**

Preparation: 1 hour Cooking: 55 minutesServings: 8
Ingredients

3 cups rolled oats

2 cups dates, pitted and chopped1 cup flaked or shredded coconut1/2 cup wheat germ
1/4 cup soy milk powder 1/2 cup almonds chopped3/4 cup honey strained
1/2 cup almond butter (plain, unsalted) softened1/4 cup peanut butter softened
Directions:

Preheat oven to 300F.

Add all ingredients into a food processor and pulse until roughlycombined.

Spread mixture evenly into greased 10 x 15-inch baking pan.Bake for 45 to 55 minutes.
Stir mixture several times during baking.

Remove from the oven and cool completely. Store in a covered glass jar.

30. Hazelnut & Maple Chia Crunch

Preparation Time: 30 Minutes Cooking Time: 5 Minutes
Servings: 2
Ingredients:

Chia Seeds (.25 C.)

Olive Oil (1 t.)

Maple Syrup (.50 C.) Hazelnuts (1.25 C.) Salt (to Taste)
Directions:
To begin this recipe, start by heating a pan over medium heat. Once

warm, place the olive oil and maple in and bring to a boil.

Once boiling, stir in your hazelnuts and cook on high for a minute or two. After this time passes, add in the chia seeds and salt and cook for another three minutes.

Now, turn the heat down to low and begin crushing the hazelnuts in the pan before pouring onto a lined cookie sheet. At this point, try to spread the mixture evenly across the pan and then place it in the freezer for 15 minutes.

Once the mixture has completely cooled, chop the ingredients into clusters and enjoy.

Nutrition: Calories: 330 Proteins: 3g Carbs: 60g Fats: 11g

Dinner Recipes

31. Butternut Squash Steak

Preparation Time: 30 min.Cooking Time: 50 min. Servings: 4

Ingredients:

2 tbsp. coconut yogurt

½ t. sweet paprika

1 ¼ c. low-sodium vegetable broth

1 sprig thyme

1 finely chopped garlic clove1 big thinly sliced shallot

1 tbsp. margarine

2 tbsp. olive oil, extra virgin Salt and pepper to liking Directions:

Bring the oven to 375 heat setting.

Cut the squash, lengthwise, into 4 steaks.

Carefully core one side of each squash with a paring knife in acrosshatch pattern.

Using a brush, coat with olive oil each side of the steak then seasongenerously with salt and pepper.

In an oven-safe, non-stick skillet, bring 2 tablespoons of olive oil to awarm temperature.

Place the steaks on the skillet with the cored side down and cook at medium temperature until browned, approximately 5 minutes.

Flip and repeat on the other side for about 3 minutes.

Place the skillet into the oven to roast the squash for 7 minutes.

Take out from the oven, placing on a plate and covering withaluminum foil to keep warm.

Using the previously used skillet, add thyme, garlic, and shallot, cooking at medium heat. Stir frequently for about 2 minutes.

Add brandy and cook for an additional minute.

Next, add paprika and whisk the mixture together for 3 minutes.Add in the yogurt seasoning with salt and pepper. Plate the steaks and spoon the sauce over the top.

Garnish with parsley and enjoy!

Nutrition: Calories: 300 | Carbohydrates: 46 g | Proteins: 5.3 g | Fats:10.6g

32. Eggplant & mushrooms in peanut sauce

Preparation time 32 minutes Cooking time: 10 minutes Servings: 6
Ingredients:

4 Japanese eggplants cut into 1-inch thick round slices

3/4 pounds of shiitake mu shrooms, stems discarded, halved3 tablespoons smooth peanut butter
2 1/2 tablespoons rice vinegar1 1/2 tablespoons soy sauce
1 1/2 tablespoons, peeled, fresh ginger, finely grated1 1/2 tablespoons light brown sugar
Coarse salt to taste

3 scallions, cut into 2-inch lengths, thinly sliced lengthwise
Direction:
Placetheeggplantsandmushroominasteamer.Steamthe eggplant and mushrooms until tender. Transfer to a bowl.

To a small bowl, add peanut butter and vinegar and whisk.

Add rest of the ingredients and whisk well. Add this to the bowl ofeggplant slices. Add scallions and mix well.

Serve hot.

33. Cassoulet

Preparation time: 35 minutes Cooking time: 1 hr and 30 minutesServings: 4

Protein content per serving: 22 gIngredients

¼ cup (60 ml) olive oil, divided

4 ounces (113 g) quit-the-cluck seitan, chopped 1/3 of a smoky sausage, chopped

1½ cups (240 g) chopped onion

2 ounces (57 g) minced shiitake mushrooms

2 large carrots, peeled, sliced into ¼-inch (6 mm) rounds2 stalks celery, chopped

1½ cups (355 ml) vegetable broth, divided

1 teaspoon liquid smoke

3 cans (each 15 ounces, or 425 g) white beans of choice, drainedand rinsed

1 can (14.5 ounces, or 410 g) diced tomatoes, undrained

2 tablespoons (32 g) tomato paste 1 tablespoon (15 ml) tamari

1 tablespoon (18 g) no chicken bouillon paste, or 2 bouillon cubes,crumbled

2 tablespoons (8 g) minced fresh parsley2 teaspoons dried thyme

½ teaspoon dried rosemary salt and pepper2 cups (200 g) fresh bread crumbs

½ cup (40 g) panko crumbsDirection

Preheat the oven to 375°f (190°c, or gas mark 5).

Heat 1 tablespoon (15 ml) of olive oil in a large skillet over medium heat.

Add the seitan and sausage. Cook for 4 to 6 minutes, occasionally stirring, until browned. Transfer to a plate and set aside.

Add the onion and a pinch of salt to the same skillet. Cook for 5 to 7 minutes until translucent. Transfer to the same plate. Add the shiitakes, carrots, and celery to the skillet and cook for 2 minutes. Add 1 tablespoon (15 ml) vegetable broth and the liquid smoke. Cook for 2 to 3 minutes, stirring until the liquid is absorbed or evaporated.

Return the seitan and onions to the skillet and add the beans, tomatoes, tomato paste, tamari, bouillon, parsley, thyme, rosemary, and remaining broth. Cook for 3 to 4 minutes, stirring to combine.

Season with salt and pepper to taste and transfer to a large casserole pan.

Toss together the fresh bread crumbs, panko crumbs, and the remaining 3 tablespoons (45 ml) olive oil in a small bowl. Spread evenly over the bean mixture. Bake for 30 to 35 minutes until the crumbs are browned.

34. Double-garlic bean and vegetable soup

Preparation time: 25 minutes Cooking time: 10 minutes Servings: 4

Protein content per serving: 21 gIngredients

1 tablespoon (15 ml) olive oil

1 teaspoon fine sea salt

1 (240 g) minced onion 5 cloves garlic, minced2 cups (220 g) chopped red potatoes

⅔ cup (96 g) sliced carrots

Protein content per serving cup (60 g) chopped celery 1 teaspoon italian seasoning blend

Protein content per serving teaspoon red pepper flakes, or to taste

Protein content per serving teaspoon celery seed 4 cups water (940 ml), divided

1 can (14.5 ounces, or 410 g) crushed tomatoes or tomato puree

1 head roasted garlic

2 tablespoons (30 g) prepared vegan pesto, plus more for garnish

2 cans (each 15 ounces, or 425 g) different kinds of white beans,drained and rinsed

Protein content per serving cup (50 g) 1-inch (2.5 cm)

pieces green beans Salt and pepper

Directions:

Heat the oil and salt in a large soup pot over medium heat. Add the onion, garlic, potatoes, carrots, and celery. Cook for 4 to 6 minutes, occasionally stirring, until the onions are translucent. Add the seasoning blend, red pepper flakes, and celery seed and stir for 2 minutes. Add 3 cups (705 ml) of the water and the crushed tomatoes.

Combine the remaining 1 cup (235 ml) water and the roasted garlic in a blender. Process until smooth. Add to the soup mixture and bring to a boil. Reduce the heat to simmer and cook for 30 minutes.

Stir in the pesto, beans, and green beans. Simmer for 15 minutes. Taste and adjust the seasonings. Serve each bowl with a dollop of pesto, if desired.

Lunch Recipes

35. Breaded Tofu Steaks

Preparation Time: 10 minutes Cooking Time: 12 minutes
Serving: 4
Ingredients:

3 cups (750 grams) tofu, extra-firm, pressed 4 tablespoons tomato paste

2 ½ tablespoons minced garlic

1 cup (236 grams) panko breadcrumbs and more as needed

½ teaspoon ground black pepper 2 tablespoon maple syrup
2 tablespoon Dijon mustard

2 tablespoon soy sauce 4 tablespoons olive oil 2 tablespoon water BBQ sauce for serving Directions:

Prepare the tofu steaks: pat dry tofu and then cut them into four slices.

Prepare the sauce: take a medium bowl, add garlic, black pepper, maple syrup, mustard, tomato paste, soy sauce, and water; stir until combined.

Take a shallow dish and place bread crumbs on it.

Working on one tofu steak at a time, first coat it with prepared sauce, then dredge it with bread crumbs until evenly coated and place it ona plate.

Repeat with the remaining tofu slices.

Take a frying pan, place it over medium heat, pour oil in it and when hot, place a tofu steak inside and cook for 4 to 6 minutes per side until golden brown and cooked.

Transfer tofu steak to a plate and repeat with the remaining tofusteaks.

Serve tofu steaks with the BBQ sauce.

Nutrition: 419.4 Cal; 23.9 g Fat; 3.9 g Saturated Fat; 33.3 g Carbs;

4.3 g Fiber; 22.8 g Protein; 3 g Sugar;

36. Quinoa Avocado Salad

Preparation Time: 15 minutes Cooking Time: 4 minutes Servings: 4

Ingredients:

2 tablespoons balsamic vinegar

¼ cup cream

¼ cup buttermilk

5 tablespoons freshly squeezed lemon juice, divided 1 clove garlic, grated

2 tablespoons shallot, mincedSalt and pepper to taste

2 tablespoons avocado oil, divided 1 ¼ cups quinoa, cooked

2 heads endive, sliced

2 firm pears, sliced thinly2 avocados, sliced

¼ cup fresh dill, chopped

Direction

Combine the vinegar, cream, milk, 1 tablespoon lemon juice, garlic,shallot, salt and pepper in a bowl.

Pour 1 tablespoon oil into a pan over medium heat. Heat the quinoa for 4 minutes.

Transfer quinoa to a plate.

Toss the endive and pears in a mixture of remaining oil, remaininglemon juice, salt and pepper.

Transfer to a plate.

Toss the avocado in the reserved dressing. Add to the plate.

Top with the dill and quinoa.

Nutrition: Calories: 431 Total fat: 28.5g Saturated fat: 8g Cholesterol: 13mg Sodium: 345mg Potassium: 779mg Carbohydrates: 42.7gFiber: 6g Sugar: 3g Protein: 6.6g

37. **Roasted Sweet Potatoes**

Preparation Time: 20 minutes Cooking Time: 20 minutes
Servings: 4
Ingredients:

2 potatoes, sliced into wedges 2 tablespoons olive oil, dividedSalt and pepper to taste

1 red bell pepper, chopped

¼ cup fresh cilantro, chopped1 garlic, minced
2 tablespoons almonds, toasted and sliced

1 tablespoon lime juiceDirection
Preheat your oven to 425 degrees F. Toss the sweet potatoes in oil and salt.Transfer to a baking pan.
Roast for 20 minutes.

In a bowl, combine the red bell pepper, cilantro, garlic and almonds. In another bowl, mix the lime juice, remaining oil, salt and pepper.
Drizzle this mixture over the red bell pepper mixture. Serve sweet potatoes with the red bell pepper mixture.

Nutrition: Calories: 146 Total fat: 8.6g Saturated fat: 1.1g Sodium: 317mg Potassium: 380mg Carbohydrates: 16g Fiber: 2.9g Sugar: 5g Protein: 2.3g

38. Roasted Tomato Sandwich

This sandwich is full of fresh ingredients, many of which cannot be prepared ahead. But, when you simply have to prepare some lettuce, an avocado, or tomato, this is not a problem. You can still have an easy and quick meal. But, that doesn't mean you can't prepare any aspects of this sandwich ahead of time. If using homemade bread, you can prepare it at the beginning of the week and store it in the cold-storage box or icebox. You can also prepare the garlic aioli ahead of time and store it in a Mason jar in the fridge.

Preparation time: 30 minutes Cooking Time: 25 minutes
Servings: 2
Ingredients:

Sourdough bread – 4 slices

Tomatoes, large, cut into eight rounds – 2Avocado – 1
Sea salt – .25 teaspoon

Vegan mayonnaise – .25 cupGarlic, minced – 2 cloves
Juice of lemon fruit – 1 tablespoon Oregano, dried – .25 teaspoon Black ground pepper – .25 teaspoonOlive oil – 2 tablespoons
Fresh basil – .25 cup

Arugula – .25 cupDirections:
Begin by setting your electric cooker to Fahrenheit 350 degrees and

lining an aluminum sheet pan with kitchen parchment.

Layout the sliced tomatoes on the sheet, and sprinkle them with part of the salt, oregano, and pepper, and allow them to roast until tender, about fifteen minutes.

Meanwhile, prepare the garlic aioli. Whisk together the mayonnaise, garlic, juice of lemon fruit, and some sea salt and pepper. Chill in the fridge until use.

Use a pastry brush and coat one side of each slice of bread with the olive oil. While doing this preheat a skillet over midway warmth. Once hot, toast the bread oil-side down until browned and then remove them from the heat.

To prepare the sandwiches, lay out the bread, oil side down. On each slice spread the garlic aioli. On half of the slices cover with the roasted tomatoes, sliced avocado, basil, and arugula. Top these slices with their matched slice without toppings. Slice the sandwiches in half before serving.

Nutrition: Calories 525

39. **Arugula and Artichokes Bowls**

Preparation time: 5 minutes Cooking time: 0 minutes
Servings: 4
Ingredients:

1 cups baby arugula

¼ cup walnuts, chopped

1 cup canned artichoke hearts, drained and quartered 1
tablespoon balsamic vinegar
2 tablespoons cilantro, chopped

2 tablespoons olive oil

Salt and black pepper to the taste1 tablespoon lemon juice
Directions:

In a bowl, combine the artichokes with the arugula,
walnuts and the other ingredients, toss, divide into smaller
bowls and serve for lunch.

Nutrition: calories 200, fat 2, fiber 1, carbs 5, protein 7

40. Minty arugula soup

Preparation time: 5 minutes Cooking time: 10 minutes
Servings: 4
Ingredients:

3 scallions, chopped 1 tablespoon olive oil
½ Cup coconut milk

2 cups baby arugula

2 tablespoons mint, chopped6 cups vegetable stock
2 tablespoons chives, chopped Salt and black pepper to the tasteDirections:

Heat up a pot with the oil over medium high heat, add the scallionsand sauté for 2 minutes.

Add the rest of the ingredients, toss, bring to a simmer and cookover medium heat for 8 minutes more.

Divide the soup into bowls and serve.

Nutrition: calories 200, fat 4, fiber 2, carbs 6, protein 10

41. Spinach and Broccoli Soup

Preparation time: 10 minutes Cooking time: 20 minutes Servings: 4
Ingredients:

3 shallots, chopped 1 tablespoon olive oil
2 garlic cloves, minced

½ pound broccoli florets

½ pound baby spinach

Salt and black pepper to the taste4 cups veggie stock
1 teaspoon turmeric powder 1 tablespoon lime juice
Directions:

Heat up a pot with the oil over medium high heat, add the shallotsand the garlic and sauté for 5 minutes.

Add the broccoli, spinach and the other ingredients, toss, bring to asimmer and cook over medium heat for 15 minutes.

Ladle into soup bowls and serve.

Nutrition: calories 150, fat 3, fiber 1, carbs 3, protein 7

42. Eggplant and Peppers Soup

Preparation time: 10 minutes Cooking time: 40 minutes Servings: 4

Ingredients:

2 red bell peppers, chopped3 scallions, chopped

3 garlic cloves, minced2 tablespoon olive oil

Salt and black pepper to the taste

5 cups vegetable stock1 bay leaf

½ cup coconut cream

1 pound eggplants, roughly cubed 2 tablespoons basil, chopped Directions:

Heat up a pot with the oil over medium heat, add the scallions andthe garlic and sauté for 5 minutes.

Add the peppers and the eggplants and sauté for 5 minutes more.

Add the remaining ingredients, toss, bring to a simmer, cook for 30minutes, ladle into bowls and serve for lunch.

Nutrition: calories 180, fat 2, fiber 3, carbs 5, protein 10

Recipes For Main Courses And Single Dishes

43. Spicy Cheesy Tofu Balls

Preparation Time: 30 minutes Cooking Time: 15 minutes
Servings: 4
Ingredients:

⅓ cup vegan mayonnaise

¼ cup pickled jalapenos1 pinch cayenne pepper

3 oz. grated vegan cheddar cheese1 tsp paprika powder
1 tbsp mustard powder

1 tbsp flax seed powder + 3 tbsp water2 ½ cup crumbled tofu
Salt and black pepper to taste

2 tbsp vegan butter, for fryingDirections:
For the spicy cheese:

In a bowl, mix all the ingredients for the spicy vegan cheese until wellcombined. Set aside.

In another medium bowl, combine the flax seed powder with waterand allow soaking for 5 minutes.

Add the flax egg to the cheese mixture, the crumbled tofu, salt, andblack pepper, and combine well. Use your hands to form large

meatballs out of the mix.

Melt the vegan butter in a large skillet over medium heat and fry thetofu balls until cooked and golden brown on all sides, 10 minutes.

Serve the tofu balls with your favorite mashes or in burgers.

44. Radish Chips

Preparation Time: 20 Minutes Cooking Time: 10 Minutes
Servings: 4
Ingredients:

10-15 Radishes, Large

Sea Salt & Black Pepper to TasteDirections:
Start by heating your oven to 375.

Slice your radishes thin, and then spread them out on a cookie sheetthat's been sprayed with cooking spray.

Mist the radishes with cooking spray, and then season with salt andpepper.

Bake for ten minutes, and then flip.

Bake for five to ten minutes more. They should be crispy.

Interesting Facts: Potatoes are a great starchy source of potassium and protein. They are pretty inexpensive if you are one that is watching their budget. Bonus: Very heart healthy!

45. Sautéed Pears

Preparation Time: 35 Minutes Cooking Time: 30 Minutes
Servings: 6
Ingredients:

2 Tablespoons Margarine (Or Vegan Butter)

¼ Teaspoon Cinnamon

¼ Teaspoon Nutmeg

6 Bosc Pears, Peeled & Quartered 1 Tablespoon Lemon
Juice
½ Cup Walnuts, Toasted & Chopped (Optional)
Directions:

Melt your vegan butter in a skillet, and then add your
spices. Cook for a half a minute before adding in your
pears.

Cook for fifteen minutes, and then stir in your lemon
juice. Serve with walnuts if desired.
Interesting Facts: Cinnamon: This spice is an absolute
powerhouse

and is considered one of the healthiest, beneficial
spices on the plant. It's widely known for its medicinal
properties. This spice is loaded with powerful antioxidants
and is popular for its anti- inflammatory properties. It can
reduce heart disease and lower bloodsugar levels.

Nutrient-Packed Protein Salads

46. Red Cabbage Salad With Curried Seitan

Preparation time: 10 mins Cooking time: 10 mins
Ingredient:

   1 Tbs. olive oil

   1 8-oz. pkg. seitan, cut into bite-size strips 3 cloves garlic, minced (1 Tbs.)
   ¾ tsp. mild curry powder

   6 cups shredded red cabbage (½ small head)

   1 small cucumber, sliced into thin half-moons (¾ cup)3 green onions, thinly sliced (½ cup)

   ⅓ cup prepared mango chutney

⅓ cup creamy natural peanut butter.

Directions:

To make Dressing: Blend chutney, peanut butter, and 1/3 cup water in blender until smooth. Set aside. To make Salad: Heat 2 tsp. oil in large skillet over medium heat. Add seitan, and season with salt, if desired. Sauté 5 to 7 minutes, or until browned. Add garlic andremaining 1 tsp. oil, and sauté 30 seconds. Sprinkle with curry powder, and sauté 2 minutes more. Remove from heat, and keep warm. Toss cabbage and cucumber with Dressing in large bowl. Topwith warm seitan and green onions.

Flavour Boosters (Fish Glazes, Meat Rubs & Fish Rubs)

47. Rosemary Thyme Rub

This special rub recipe represents an interesting balance of spicy and sweet flavors to make truly mesmerizing meat meals.

A spiced combo of rosemary, thyme, and celery seeds never fails to produce delicious dishes with well-balanced flavors for the whole family.

Preparation Time: 5 min.

Cooking Time: 5 min. Servings: 1 cup/16 tbs.Ingredients: Dried thyme - 1/4 cup

Dried crushed rosemary - 1/4 cupDry mustard - 2 tbs. Ground black pepper - 4 tsp.Salt - 4 tsp.

Onion powder - 4 tsp.Ground cloves - 2 tsp.Celery seed - 2 tsp.

Cayenne- 1 tsp.Directions:

Mix in all mentioned rub ingredients in your mixing bowl to make the rosemary rub. Gently mix all ingredients using spatula or spoon to form an aromatic rub mixture.

Now, take your choice of meat cut and place it on a firm surface. Brush the freshly made rub on it; pat gently for the rub to stick onto the surface. Turn the meat cut and repeat to spice up its other side. Repeat with other meat cuts.

Let your meat cuts adequately season for more rich flavors for a few hours in your refrigerator. Take them out, as they are ready to be cooked or grilled!

48. Super Spiced Curry Rub

Your favorite meat cuts deserve a little jazzing up with this unique curry flavored rub. Paprika mixed with curry powder and cinnamon creates a perfect blend of spices. Be creative and add one or two of your favorite spices in it to come up with your own special version of spiced curry rub.

Preparation Time: 5 min.Cooking Time: 5 min.
Yield: 10 tbs.

Ingredients:

Ground ginger - 2 tbs.

Yellow curry powder - 3 tbs.Ground cinnamon - 2 tbs.
Salt - 1 tsp.

Mild paprika - 1 tbs. Ground cumin - 2 tbs. Ground allspice - 1 tsp.Directions:

One by one, mix in all mentioned rub ingredients in your mixing bowl to make the curry rub. Gently mix all the ingredients using spatula or spoon to form an aromatic rub mixture.

Now, take your choice of meat cut and place it on a firm surface. Brush or rub the freshly made rub on it; pat gently for the rub to stick to the surface. Turn the meat cut and repeat to spice up its other side. Repeat with other meat cuts.

Let your meat cuts adequately season for more rich flavors for a few hours in your refrigerator. Take them out, as they are ready to be cooked or grilled!

Sauce Recipes

49. Vegan White Bean Gravy

Preparation time: 5 minutes Cooking time: 5 minutes Servings: 2 1/5 cups Ingredients:

1 cup of soy milk

1 cup vegetable broth

1 cup white beans, rinsed and drained

1 tablespoon nutritional yeast3 tablespoons tamari

1 teaspoon garlic granules, dried

2 teaspoons onion granules, dried 2 tablespoons all-purpose flour

1 tablespoon combination thyme, oregano, dill, minced

1/4 teaspoon black pepper 1/4 teaspoon Himalayan salt Directions:

Add all ingredients except flour, herbs, and salt to a blender andblend on high speed until smooth.

Add this mixture to a pan placed over medium heat. Add salt, herbs, and flour, whisk all the time — Cook for 5 minutes.Serve and enjoy.

50. Tahini Maple Dressing

Preparation time: 5 minutes Cooking time: 5 minutes Servings: 4 oz
Ingredients

¼ cup tahini

1 ½ tablespoons maple syrup2 teaspoons lemon juice
¼ cup of water

1/8 teaspoon Himalayan pink saltDirections:

Add all the ingredients to a bowl, Stir well to combine, until wellmixed.

Use as a dressing for the salad or other dishes. Store in a fridge.

Plant Based Diet Cookbook 2021

2 Books in 1: A Collection of 100+ Healthy Plant-Based Recipes for Losing Weight and Feeling Great

Frank Smith

Breakfasts

51. Onion & Mushroom Tart with a Nice Brown Rice Crust

Preparation 10 minutesCooking 55 minutes Serving: 1
Ingredients:

1 ½ pounds, mushrooms, button, portabella,1 cup, short-grain brown rice
2 ¼ cups, water

½ teaspoon, ground black pepper 2 teaspoons, herbal spice blend 1 sweet large onion 7 ounces, extra-firm tofu

1 cup, plain non-dairy milk 2 teaspoons, onion powder
2 teaspoons, low-sodium soy1 teaspoon, molasses
¼ teaspoon, ground turmeric ¼ cup, white wine

¼ cup, tapiocaDirections:
Cook the brown rice and put it aside for later use.

Slice the onions into thin strips and sauté them in water until they are soft. Then, add the molasses, and cook them for a few minutes.

Next, sauté the mushrooms in water with the herbal spice blend. Once the mushrooms are cooked and they are soft, add the white wine or sherry. Cook everything for a few more minutes.

In a blender, combine milk, tofu, arrowroot, turmeric, and onion powder till you have a smooth mixture

On a pie plate, create a layer of rice, spreading evenly to form a crust. The rice should be warm and not cold. It will be easy to work with warm rice. You can also use a pastry roller to get an even crust. With your fingers, gently press the sides.

Take half of the tofu mixture and the mushrooms and spoon them over the tart dish. Smooth the level with your spoon.

Now, top the layer with onions followed by the tofu mixture. You can smooth the surface again with your spoon.

Sprinkle some black pepper on top.

Bake the pie at 350o F for about 45 minutes. Toward the end, you can cover it loosely with tin foil. This will help the crust to remain moist.

Allow the pie crust to cool down, so that you can slice it. If you are in love with vegetarian dishes, there is no way that you will not love thispie.

Nutrition: Calories: 245.3, Fats 16.4 g, Proteins 6.8 g, Carbohydrates 18.3 g

52. **Perfect Breakfast Shake**

Preparation: 5 minutesCooking: 0 minutes Servings: 2
Ingredients:

3 tablespoons, raw cacao powder1 cup, almond milk

2 frozen bananas

3 tablespoons, natural peanut butterDirections:
Use a powerful blender to combine all the ingredients.
Process everything until you have a smooth shake.
Enjoy a hearty shake to kickstart your day.

Nutrition: Calories: 330, Fats 15 g, Carbohydrates 41 g, Proteins 11g

53. Beet Gazpacho

Preparation time: 10 minutes Cooking time: 2 minutes
Servings: 4
Ingredients:

½ large bunch young beets with stems, roots and leaves 2 small cloves garlic, peeled,
Salt to taste

Pepper to taste

½ teaspoon liquid stevia 1 glass coconut milk kefir 1 teaspoon chopped dill
½ tablespoon canola oil

1 small red onion, chopped

1 tablespoon apple cider vinegar 2 cups vegetable broth or water 1 tablespoon chopped chives
1 scallion, sliced Roasted baby potatoes Directions:
Cut the roots and stems of the beets into small pieces. Thinly slice the beet greens.

Place a saucepan over medium heat. Add oil. When the oil is heated, add onion and garlic and cook until onion turns translucent.

Stir in the beets, roots and stem and cook for a minute.

Add broth, salt and water and cover with a lid. Simmer until tender.

Add stevia and vinegar and mix well. Taste and adjust the

stevia andvinegar if required.

Turn off the heat. Blend with an immersion blender until smooth.

Place the saucepan back over it. When it begins to boil, add beetgreens and cook for a minute. Turn off the heat.

Cool completely. Chill if desired. Add rest of the ingredients and stir.
Serve in bowls with roasted potatoes if desired.

Nutrition: Calories 101, Fats 5 g, Carbohydrates 14 g, Proteins 2 g

54. Healthy Breakfast Bowl

Preparation: 10 mCooking: 10 m Ingredients:

1 vegan yogurt 1/2 avocado (peeled and diced) 1 handful blueberries 1 tablespoon cacao nibs 1 handful of strawberries 1 tablespoon mulberries 1 tablespoon goji berries tablespoon desiccated coconut

2 Directions:

Put the avocado in a nice bowl. Top up with vegan yogurt.

Sprinkle the remaining ingredients and enjoy it.

Nutrition: carbohydrates: 55 g calories: 471 Fat: 25g sodium: 183 gprotein: 11 g sugar: 32 g

55. Pumpkin Pancakes

Preparation time: 15 minutes Cooking time: 15 minutes Servings: 4

Ingredients

2 cups unsweetened almond milk 1 teaspoon apple cider vinegar 2½ cups whole-wheat flour

2 tablespoons baking powder

½ Teaspoon baking soda1 teaspoon sea salt

1 teaspoon pumpkin pie spice or ½ teaspoon ground cinnamon plus¼ teaspoon grated nutmeg plus ¼ teaspoon ground allspice½ Cup canned pumpkin purée 1 cup water tablespoon coconut oilDirections

In a small bowl, combine the almond milk and apple cider vinegar.Set aside.

In a bowl, whisk together the flour, baking powder, baking soda, salt,and pumpkin pie spice. In bowl, combine the almond milk mixture, pumpkin purée, and water, whisking to mix well. Mix the wet Ingredients to the dry Ingredients and fold together until the dry- Ingredients are just moistened.

In a nonstick pan or griddle over medium-high heat, melt the coconut oil and swirl to coat. Pour the batter into the pan ¼ cup at a time and cook until the pancakes are browned, about 5 minutes per side. Serve immediately.

56. Green Breakfast Smoothie

Preparation: 10 minutesCooking: 0 minutes Servings: 2
Ingredients

½ Banana, sliced cups spinach or other greens, such as kale 1 cup sliced berries of your choosing, fresh or frozen
1 orange, peeled and cut into segments
1 cup unsweetened nondairy milk cup ice Directions
In a blender, combine all the Ingredients.

Starting with the blender on low speed, begin blending the smoothie, gradually increasing blender speed until smooth. Serve immediately.

57. **Blueberry And Chia Smoothie**

Preparation: 10 minutesCooking: 0 minutes Servings: 2
Ingredients

1 tablespoons chia seeds 2 cups unsweetened nondairy milk 2 cups blueberries, fresh or frozen 2 tablespoons pure maple syrup or agave2 tablespoons cocoa powder
Directions:

Soak the chia seeds in the almond milk for 5 minutes.

In a blender, combine the soaked chia seeds, almond milk, blueberries, maple syrup, and cocoa powder and blend until smooth.Serve immediately.

58. Berries with Mascarpone on Toasted Bread

Preparation Time: 10 minutes Cooking Time: 0 minute
Servings: 1
Ingredients:

1 slice whole-wheat bread

2 tablespoons mascarpone cheese1/8 cup raspberries
1/8 cup strawberries

1 teaspoon fresh mint leavesDirections:
Spread the cheese on the bread.

Top with the berries and chopped mint leaves. Store in food container and refrigerate.
Toast in the oven when ready to eat.

Nutrition: Calories: 326 fat: 27.3g Saturated fat: 14.2g Cholesterol: 70mg Sodium: 130mg Potassium: 115mg Carbohydrates: 15.1g Fiber: 4.1g Sugar: 3g Protein: 7.9g

59. Fruit Cup

Preparation Time: 15 minutes Cooking Time: 0 minute Servings: 4Ingredients:

2 cups melon, sliced

2 cups strawberries, sliced 2 cups grapes, sliced in half 2 cups peaches, sliced

3 tablespoons freshly squeezed lime juice

½ teaspoon ground ginger1 tablespoon honey

3 teaspoons lime zest

¼ cup coconut flakes, toastedDirections:

Toss the fruits in lime juice, ginger and honey.Sprinkle the lime zest on top.

Top with the coconut flakes.

Nutrition: Calories: 65 Total fat: 1.3g Saturated fat: 1.1g Sodium: 20mg Potassium: 247mg Carbohydrates: 13.9g Fiber: 1.6g Sugar: 10g Protein: 1g

60. Oatmeal with Black Beans & Cheddar

Preparation Time: 10 minutes Cooking Time: 0 minute
Servings: 2
Ingredients:

½ cup rolled oats

¼ cup Vegan yogurt

½ cup almond milk

2 tablespoons seasoned black beans

2 tablespoons Cheddar cheese, shredded 1 stalk scallion, minced 1 tablespoon cilantro, chopped

Directions:

Mix all the ingredients except the cilantro in a glass jar with lid.Refrigerate for up to 5 days.
Sprinkle the cilantro on top before serving.

Nutrition: Calories: 47 Total fat: 1.2g Saturated fat: 0.5g Sodium: 30mg Potassium: 151mg Carbohydrates: 11g Fiber: 1.9g Sugar: 9g Protein: 2g

61. Strawberry Smoothie Bowl

Preparation time: 30 minutes Cooking time: 0 minutes Servings: 02
Ingredients:

Smoothie bowl:

1½ cups frozen strawberries

½ cup coconut milkChia seeds Directions:
In a blender jug, puree all the ingredients for the smooth bowl.Pour the smoothie in the serving bowl.

Add strawberries, banana and chia seeds on top.Chill well then serve.

Nutrition: Calories 275 Total Fat 14.5 g Saturated Fat 12.5 g

Cholesterol 36 mg Sodium 13 mg Total Carbs 25 g Fiber 5 g Sugar 5

g Protein 2.5 g

Soups, Salads, and Sides

62. Creamy Squash Soup

Preparation time: 35 minutes Cooking time: 22 minutes
Servings: 8
Ingredients:

3 cups butternut squash, chopped

1 ½ cups unsweetened coconut milk1 tbsp coconut oil
1 tsp dried onion flakes1 tbsp curry powder
4 cups water

1 garlic clove

1 tsp kosher saltDirections:
Add squash, coconut oil, onion flakes, curry powder, water, garlic,and salt into a large saucepan. Bring to boil over high heat.

Turn heat to medium and simmer for 20 minutes.

Puree the soup using a blender until smooth. Return soup to the saucepan and stir in coconut milk and cook for 2 minutes.

Stir well and serve hot.

Nutrition: calories 146; fat 12.6 g; carbohydrates 9.4 g; sugar 2.8 g;

protein 1.7 g; cholesterol 0 mg

63. Cucumber Edamame Salad

Preparation time: 5 minutes Cooking time: 8 minutes
Servings: 2
Ingredients:

3 tbsp. Avocado oil

1 cup cucumber, sliced into thin rounds

½ cup fresh sugar snap peas, sliced or whole

½ cup fresh edamame

¼ cup radish, sliced

1 large avocado, peeled, pitted, sliced 1 nori sheet,
crumbled
2 tsp. Roasted sesame seeds1 tsp. Salt
Directions:

Bring a medium-sized pot filled halfway with water to
a boil overmedium-high heat.

Add the sugar snaps and cook them for about 2 minutes.

Take the pot off the heat, drain the excess water, transfer
the sugarsnaps to a medium-sized bowl and set aside for
now.

Fill the pot with water again, add the teaspoon of salt
and bring to aboil over medium-high heat.

Add the edamame to the pot and let them cook for about

6 minutes.

Take the pot off the heat, drain the excess water, transfer the soybeans to the bowl with sugar snaps and let them cool down for about 5 minutes.

Combine all ingredients, except the nori crumbs and roasted sesameseeds, in a medium-sized bowl.

Carefully stir, using a spoon, until all ingredients are evenly coated in oil. Top the salad with the nori crumbs and roasted sesame seeds.

Transfer the bowl to the fridge and allow the salad to cool for at least30 minutes.

Serve chilled and enjoy!

Nutrition: Calories 409 Carbohydrates 7.1 g Fats 38.25 g Protein 7.6g

64. **Best Broccoli Salad**

Preparation time: 15 minutes Chilling time: 1 hour
Servings: 8
Ingredients:

8 cups diced broccoli

¼ cup sunflower seeds

3 tablespoons apple cider vinegar

½ cup dried cranberries1/3 cup cubed onion
1 cup mayonnaise

½ cup bacon bits

2 tablespoons sugar

½ teaspoon salt and ground black pepperDirections:
In a bowl, mix vinegar, salt, pepper, mayonnaise, and
sugar. Mix it

well. In another bowl, mix all the remaining ingredients
and pour the prepared mayonnaise dressing and mix it
well. Before serving to refrigerate it for at least an hour.

Nutrition: Carbohydrates 17g, protein 6g, fats 26g, calories
317

Entrées

65. Crunchy Asparagus Spears

Preparation time: 25 minutes Cooking time: 25 minutes
Servings: 4
Ingredients:

1 bunch asparagus spears (about 12 spears)

¼ cup nutritional yeast

2 tablespoons hemp seeds1 teaspoon garlic powder
¼ teaspoon paprika (or more if you like paprika)

⅛ teaspoon ground pepper

¼ cup whole-wheat breadcrumbsJuice of ½ lemon
Directions:

Preheat the oven to 350 degrees, Fahrenheit.   Line

Wash the asparagus, snapping off the white part at

the bottom.Save it for making vegetable stock.

Mix together the nutritional yeast, hemp seed, garlic powder, paprika,pepper and breadcrumbs.

Place asparagus spears on the baking sheets giving them a little room in between and sprinkle with the mixture in the bowl.

Bake for up to 25 minutes, until crispy.

Serve with lemon juice if desired.

66. Cucumber Bites with Chive and Sunflower Seeds

Preparation time: 5 minutes Cooking time: 5 minutes Servings: 2
Ingredients:

1 cup raw sunflower seed ½ teaspoon salt

½ cup chopped fresh chives1 clove garlic, chopped
2 tablespoons red onion, minced

2 tablespoons lemon juice

½ cup water (might need more or less)4 large cucumbers
Directions:

Place the sunflower seeds and salt in the food processor and process to a fine powder. It will take only about 10 seconds.

Add the chives, garlic, onion, lemon juice and water and process until creamy, scraping down the sides frequently. The mixture shouldbe very creamy; if not, add a little more water.

Cut the cucumbers into 1½-inch coin-like pieces.

Spread a spoonful of the sunflower mixture on top and set on a platter. Sprinkle more chopped chives on top and refrigerate until

ready to serve.

Smoothies and Beverages

67. Tangy Spiced Cranberry Drink

Preparation time: 3 hours and 10 minutes Cooking time: 3 hours

Servings: 14

Ingredients:

1 1/2 cups of coconut sugar 12 whole cloves

2 fluid ounce of lemon juice

6 fluid ounce of orange juice

32 fluid ounce of cranberry juice 8 cups of hot water
1/2 cup of Red Hot candies

Directions:

Pour the water into a 6-quarts slow cooker along with the cranberry juice, orange juice, and the lemon juice.

Stir the sugar properly.

Wrap the whole cloves in a cheese cloth, tie its corners with strings,and immerse it in the liquid present inside the slow cooker.

Add the red hot candies to the slow cooker and cover it with the lid.

Then plug in the slow cooker and let it cook on the low heat settingfor 3 hours or until it is heated thoroughly.

When done, discard the cheesecloth bag and serve.

Nutrition: Calories:89 Cal, Carbohydrates:27g, Protein:0g, Fats:0g,Fiber:1g.

68. **Warm Pomegranate Punch**

Preparation: 3 hours and 15 minutes Cooking: 3 hours Servings: 10

Ingredients:

3 cinnamon sticks, each about 3 inches long 12 whole cloves
1/2 cup of coconut sugar 1/3 cup of lemon juice

32 fluid ounce of pomegranate juice

32 fluid ounce of apple juice, unsweetened 16 fluid ounce of brewed tea
Directions:

Using a 4-quart slow cooker, pour the lemon juice, pomegranate, juice apple juice, tea, and then sugar.

Wrap the whole cloves and cinnamon stick in a cheese cloth, tie its corners with a string, and immerse it in the liquid present in the slow cooker.

Then cover it with the lid, plug in the slow cooker and let it cook atthe low heat setting for 3 hours or until it is heated thoroughly.

When done, discard the cheesecloth bag and serve it hot or cold.

Nutrition: Calories:253 Cal, Carbohydrates:58g, Protein:7g, Fats:2g,Fiber:3g.

69. **Rich Truffle Hot Chocolate**

Preparation time: 2 hours and 10 minutes Cooking time: 2 hours

Servings: 4

Ingredients:

1/3 cup of cocoa powder, unsweetened 1/3 cup of coconut sugar 1/8 teaspoon of salt

1/8 teaspoon of ground cinnamon

1 teaspoon of vanilla extract, unsweetened 32 fluid ounce of coconut milk

Directions:

Using a 2 quarts slow cooker, add all the ingredients and stir properly.

Cover it with the lid, then plug in the slow cooker and cook it for 2 hours on the high heat setting or until it is heated thoroughly.

When done, serve right away.

Nutrition: Calories:67 Cal, Carbohydrates:13g, Protein:2g, Fats:2g, Fiber:2.3g.

70. Vanilla Milkshake

Preparation: 5 min.Cooking: 5 min.Servings: 4

Ingredients:

2 c. ice cubes 2 t. vanilla extract

6 tbsp. powdered erythritol1 c. cream of dairy-free

½ c. coconut milkDirections:

In a high-speed blender, add all the ingredients and blend. Add ice cubes and blend until smooth.

Serve immediately and enjoy!

Nutrition: Calories: 125 | Carbohydrates: 6.8 g | Proteins: 1.2 g |Fats: 11.5 g

71. **Raspberry Protein Shake**

Preparation: 5 min. Cooking: 5 min.Serving: 1 Ingredients: ¼ avocado 1 c. raspberries, frozen1 scoop protein powder ½ c. almond milk

Ice cubes Directions:

In a high-speed blender add all the ingredients and blend until lumpsof fruit disappear.

Add two to four ice cubes and blend to your desired consistency.Serve immediately and enjoy!

Nutrition: Calories: 756 | Carbohydrates: 80.1 g | Proteins: 27.6 g |

Fats: 40.7 g

72. Raspberry Almond Smoothie

Preparation: 5 min.Cooking: 5 min.Serving: 1

Ingredients:

10 Almonds, finely chopped3 tbsp. almond butter
1 c. almond milk 1 c. Raspberries, frozenDirections:
In a high-speed blender, add all the ingredients and blend until

smooth.

Serve immediately and enjoy!

Nutrition: Calories: 449 | Carbohydrates: 26 g | Proteins: 14 g | Fats:35 g

73.　　Apple Raspberry Cobbler

Preparation Time: 50 minutesServings: 4

A safer type of fruit cobbler where a cut in sugar enhances the fruit.Ingredients

3 apples, peeled, cored, and chopped 2 tbsp pure date sugar cup fresh raspberries

1 tbsp unsalted plant butter

½ cup whole-wheat flour 1 cup toasted rolled oats 2 tbsp pure date sugar 1 tsp cinnamon powderDirections

Preheat the oven to 350 F and grease a baking dish with some plantbutter.

Add the apples, date sugar, and 3 tbsp of water to a medium pot. Cook over low heat until the date sugar melts and then, mix in the raspberries. Cook until the fruits soften, 10 minutes.

Pour and spread the fruit mixture into the baking dish and set aside. In a blender, add the plant butter, flour, oats, date sugar, andcinnamon powder. Pulse a few times until crumbly.

Spoon and spread the mixture on the fruit mix until evenly layered. Bake in the oven for 25 to 30 minutes or until golden brown on top. Remove the dessert, allow cooling for 2 minutes, and serve.

Nutritional info per serving

Calories 539 | Fats 12g| Carbs 105.7g | Protein 8.2g

Snacks and Desserts

74. Simple Banana Fritters

Preparation time: 15 mins Cooking time: 20 mins Servings: 8

Ingredients 4 Bananas

3 Tbsps. Maple Syrup

¼ Tsp. Cinnamon Powder

¼ Tsp. Nutmeg

1 Cup Coconut Flour Directions
Preheat oven to 350° F.

Mash the bananas in a large mixing bowl along with maple syrup, cinnamon, nutmeg powder and coconut flour.

Mix all the ingredients well.

Take 2 tbsps. mixture and make small 1-inch-thick

fritters from thismixture.

Place fritters in greased baking tray.

Bake fritters in preheated oven for about 10-15 minutes until goldenfrom both sides.

Once done, take them out of the oven.Serve with coconut cream.

Enjoy!

Nutrition: Protein: 3% 3 kcal Fat: 28% 30 kcal Carbohydrates: 69%

75 kcal

75. Coconut And Blueberries Ice Cream

Preparation time: 5 minsCooking time: 0 mins Servings: 4
Ingredients

1/4 Cup Coconut Cream1 Tbsp. Maple Syrup
¼ Cup Coconut Flour

1 Cup Blueberries

¼ Cup Blueberries For ToppingDirections
Put ingredients into food processor and mix well on high
speed.

Pour mixture in silicon molds and freeze in freezer
for about 2-4hours.

Once balls are set remove from freezer.Top with berries.
Serve cold and enjoy!

Nutrition: Protein: 3% 4 kcal Fat: 40% 60 kcal
Carbohydrates: 57%

86 kcal

76. Peach Crockpot Pudding

Preparation time: 15 mins Cooking time: 4 hours Servings: 6

Ingredients

2 Cups Sliced Peaches 1/4 Cup Maple Syrup
1/2 Tsp. Cinnamon Powder

2 Cups Coconut Milk For Serving
½ Cup Coconut Cream 1 Oz. Coconut Flakes Directions
Lightly grease the crockpot and place peaches in the bottom. Add maple syrup, cinnamon powder and milk.
Cover and cook on high for 4 hours.

Once cooked remove from crockpot. For serving pour coconut cream.
Top with coconut flakes. Serve and enjoy!
Nutrition: Protein: 3% 11 kcal Fat: 61% 230 kcal Carbohydrates: 36%

133 kcal

77. **Green Soy Beans Hummus**

Preparation time: 15 minutes Cooking time: 0 minutes Servings: 6

Ingredients

1 1/2 cups frozen green soybeans4 cups of water coarse salt to taste

1/4 cup sesame paste 1/2 tsp grated lemon peel3 Tbsp fresh lemon juice 2 cloves of garlic crushed1/2 tsp ground cumin

1/4 tsp ground coriander

4 Tbsp extra virgin olive oil

1 Tbsp fresh parsley leaves chopped

Serving options: sliced cucumber, celery, olivesDirections:

1. In a saucepan, bring to boil 4 cups of water with 2 to 3 pinch ofcoarse salt.

2. Add in frozen soybeans, and cook for 5 minutes or until tender.

3. Rinse and drain soybeans into a colander.

4. Add soybeans and all remaining ingredients into a food processor.

5. Pulse until smooth and creamy.

6. Taste and adjust salt to taste.

7. Serve with sliced cucumber, celery, olives, bread...etc.

78. **High Protein Avocado Guacamole**

Preparation time: 15 minutes Cooking time: 0 minutes
Servings: 4
Ingredients

1/2 cup of onion, finely chopped

1 chili pepper (peeled and finely chopped) 1 cup tomato,
finely chopped Cilantro leaves, fresh2 avocados

2 Tbsp linseed oil 1/2 cup ground walnuts1/2 lemon (or
lime) Salt

Directions:

Chop the onion, chili pepper, cilantro, and tomato;
place in a largebowl.

Slice avocado, open vertically, and remove the pit. Using
the spoon take out the avocado flesh.
Mash the avocados with a fork and add into the
bowl with onionmixture.

Add all remaining ingredients and stir well until
ingredients combinewell.

Taste and adjust salt and lemon/lime juice.

Keep refrigerated into covered glass bowl up to 5 days.

79. Homemade Energy Nut Bars

Preparation time: 15 minutes Cooking time: 0 minutes
Servings: 4
Ingredients

1/2 cup peanuts1 cup almonds
1/2 cup hazelnut, chopped

1 cup shredded coconut1 cup almond butter
2 tsp sesame seeds toasted

1/2 cup coconut oil, freshly melted2 Tbsp organic honey
1/4 tsp cinnamon

Directions

Add all nuts into a food processor and pulse for 1-2 minutes.

Add in shredded coconut, almond butter, sesame seeds, meltedcoconut oil, cinnamon, and honey; process only for one minute.

Cover a square plate/tray with parchment paper and apply the nutmixture.

Spread mixture vigorously with a spatula. Place in the freezer for 4 hours or overnight.

Remove from the freezer and cut into rectangular bars.

Ready! Enjoy!

80. Chocolate Energy Snack Bar

Preparation Time: 5 MinutesCooking Time: 0 Minutes

Servings: 4Ingredients:

Flax Seeds (1 T.)

Chia Seeds (1 T.) Agave Nectar (2 T.)Almonds (1 C.)
Dried Cranberries (1 C.)Dates (1 C.)
Directions:

When you need a snack that is easy to grab when you are on the go, this is the perfect recipe. You are going to start out by pulsing the almonds and dates in a food processor. Once they are chopped fine, add in the seeds, agave, and cranberries. At this point, pulse until everything is combined.

Next, you will want to add the batter into a lined pan and press everything down into the bottom.

Finally, pop the dish into the fridge for two hours, cut into squares, and your bars are ready!

Nutrition: Calories: 400 Proteins: 10g Carbs: 55g Fats: 20g

81. Zesty Orange Muffins

Preparation Time: 40 Minutes Cooking Time: 20 Minutes
Servings: 11
Ingredients:

Chopped Hazelnuts (3 T.)Orange Juice (1 C.)
Olive Oil (.50 C.)

Baking Powder (2 t.) Brown Sugar (.75 C.)Flour (2 C.)
Baking Soda (1 Pinch)Salt (to Taste)
Orange Zest (2 T.)

Directions:

Muffins are the perfect snack to grab and go when you need to leave the house quickly. Start off by prepping the oven to 350.

As this warms up, take out your mixing bowl and combine the hazelnuts, salt, baking soda, baking powder, sugar, and flour. Once these are mixed together well, add in the olive oil and orange juice.

With your mixture made, evenly pour into lined muffin tins and then pop it into the oven for 20 minutes.

By the end, the muffins should be cooked through and golden at the top. If they look done, remove from the oven, and your snack isready to go.

Nutrition: Calories: 220 Proteins: 3g Carbs: 30g Fats: 10g

82. **Chocolate Tahini Balls**

Preparation Time: 10 Minutes Cooking Time: 0 Minutes
Servings: 8
Ingredients:

Sesame Seeds (2 T.)Tahini (2 T.)

Cacao Nibs (2 T.)

Unsweetened Cocoa Powder (2 T.) Old-fashioned Rolled
Oats (.25 C.)Medjool Dates (4)
Rock Salt (1 Pinch)Directions:

For this quick snack, start off by placing all of the
ingredients aboveinto a blender and blend until you get a
dough-like texture.

Next, take the dough and mold it into 8 balls.

Place the balls in the fridge, allow to firm up for 20
minutes, and thenthey will be set.

Nutrition: Calories: 70 Proteins: 2g Carbs: 9g Fats: 4g

Dinner Recipes

83. Piquillo Salsa Verde Steak

Preparation Time: 30 min.Cooking Time: 25 min.
Yields: 8 Servings

Ingredients:

4 – ½ inch thick slices of ciabatta18 oz. firm tofu, drained
5 tbsp. olive oil, extra virgin

Pinch of cayenne

½ t. cumin, ground

1 ½ tbsp. sherry vinegar1 shallot, diced
8 piquillo peppers (can be from a jar) – drained and cut to ½ inchstrips

3 tbsp. of the following:

parsley, finely chopped capers, drained and chopped
Directions:

Place the tofu on a plate to drain the excess liquid, and then sliceinto 8 rectangle pieces.

You can either prepare your grill or use a grill pan. If using a grill pan,preheat the grill pan.

Mix 3 tablespoons of olive oil, cayenne, cumin, vinegar, shallot, parsley, capers, and piquillo peppers in a medium bowl to make our salsa verde. Season to preference with salt and pepper.

Using a paper towel, dry the tofu slices.

Brush olive oil on each side, seasoning with salt and pepper lightly.

Place the bread on the grill and toast for about 2 minutes usingmedium-high heat.

Next, grill the tofu, cooking each side for about 3 minutes or until thetofu is heated through.

Place the toasted bread on the plate then the tofu on top of thebread.

Gently spoon out the salsa verde over the tofu and serve.

Nutrition: Calories: 427 | Carbohydrates: 67.5 g | Proteins: 14.2 g |Fats: 14.6 g

84. Sweet 'n spicy tofu

Preparation time 45 minutes Cooking time: 10 minutes Servings: 8
Ingredients:

14 ounces extra firm tofu; press the excess liquid and chop intocubes.

3 tablespoons olive oil

2 2-3 cloves garlic, minced

4 tablespoons sriracha sauce or any other hot sauce 2 tablespoons soy sauce
1/4 cup sweet chili sauce

5-6 cups mixed vegetables of your choice (like carrots, cauliflower,broccoli, potato, etc.)

Salt to taste (optional)Direction:
Place a nonstick pan over medium-high heat. Add 1 tablespoon oil.

When oil is hot, add garlic and mixed vegetables and stir-fry until crisp and tender. Remove and keep aside.

Place the pan back on heat. Add 2 tablespoons oil. When oil is hot, add tofu and sauté until golden brown. Add the sautéed vegetables. Mix well and remove from heat.

Make a mixture of sauces by mixing together all the sauces in asmall bowl.

Serve the stir fried vegetables and tofu with sauce.

Lunch Recipes

85. Green Pea Fritters

Preparation Time: 10 minutes Cooking Time: 25 minutes
Serving: 4
Ingredients:

For the Fritters:

1 ½ cups (140 grams) chickpea flour 2 cups (250 grams)
frozen peas
1 large white onion, peeled, diced

1 tablespoon minced garlic 1/8 teaspoon salt
1 teaspoon baking soda

2 tablespoons mixed dried Italian herbs 1 tablespoon olive
oil
Water as needed

For the Yoghurt Sauce:

1/2 teaspoon dried rosemary 1/2 teaspoon dried parsley 1/2 teaspoon dried mint

1 lemon, juiced 1 cup soy yogurtDirections:

Switch on the oven, set it to 350° F and let it preheat.

Take a medium saucepan, place it over medium heat, add peas, cover them with water, bring it to a boil, cook for 2 to 3 minutes until tender, and when done, drain the peas and set aside until required.

Take a frying pan, place it over medium heat, add oil and when hot, add onion and garlic; cook for 5 minutes until softened.

Transfer onion-garlic mixture to a food processor, add peas and pulse for 1 minute until the thick paste comes together.

Tip the mixture in a bowl, add salt, baking soda, Italian herbs, and chickpea flour, stir until incorporated and shape the mixture into ten patties.

Brush the patties with oil, arrange them onto a baking sheet and bake for 15 to 18 minutes until golden brown and thoroughly cooked, turning halfway.

Meanwhile, prepare the yogurt sauce: take a medium bowl, add all the ingredients for it and whisk until combined.

Serve fritters with prepared yogurt sauce.

Nutrition: 94 Cal; 2 g Fat; 0 g Saturated Fat; 14 g Carbs; 3 g Fiber; 4 g Protein; 2 g Sugar

86. **Broccoli Rabe**

Preparation Time: 15 minutes Cooking Time: 15 minutes
Servings: 8
Ingredients:

2 oranges, sliced in half1 lb. broccoli rabe
2 tablespoons sesame oil, toasted

Salt and pepper to taste

1 tablespoon sesame seeds, toastedDirection
Pour the oil into a pan over medium heat.

Add the oranges and cook until caramelized.Transfer to a plate.
Put the broccoli in the pan and cook for 8 minutes.
Squeeze the oranges to release juice in a bowl.
Stir in the oil, salt and pepper.

Coat the broccoli rabe with the mixture.Sprinkle seeds on top.
Nutrition: Calories: 59 Total fat: 4.4g   Saturated fat: 0.6g Sodium:

164mg   Potassium: 160mg Carbohydrates: 4.1g Fiber: 1.6g Sugar:2g Protein: 2.2g

87. Whipped Potatoes

Preparation Time: 20 minutes Cooking Time: 35 minutes
Servings: 10
Ingredients:

4 cups water

3 lb. potatoes, sliced into cubes 3 cloves garlic, crushed
6 tablespoons vegan butter 2 bay leaves
10 sage leaves

½ cup Vegan yogurt

¼ cup low-fat milk Salt to taste Direction
Boil the potatoes in water for 30 minutes or until tender.
Drain.
In a pan over medium heat, cook the garlic in butter for 1
minute.

Add the sage and cook for 5 more minutes. Discard the
garlic.
Use a fork to mash the potatoes.

Whip using an electric mixer while gradually adding the
butter, yogurt, and milk.
Season with salt.

Nutrition: Calories: 169 Total fat: 7.6g Saturated fat: 4.7g
Cholesterol: 21mg Sodium: 251mg Potassium: 519mg
Carbohydrates: 22.1g Fiber: 1.5g Sugar: 2g Protein: 4.2g

88. Chickpea Avocado Sandwich

You can make the chickpea and avocado filling ahead of time and store it in the cold-storage box for or in the icebox. While avocado does brown easily, the lime juice helps preserve the integrity of it.

Preparation time: 10 minutes Cooking Time: 5 minutes Servings: 2
Ingredients: Chickpeas – 1 canAvocado – 1
Dill, dried – .25 teaspoon Onion powder – .25 teaspoon Sea salt – .5 teaspoon Celery, chopped – .25 cup
Green onion, chopped – .25 cup Lime juice – 3 tablespoons Garlic powder – .5 teaspoon Dark pepper, ground – dash Tomato, sliced – 1
Lettuce – 4 leavesBread – 4 slices Directions:

Drain the canned chickpeas and rinse them under cool water. Place them in a bowl along with the herbs, spices, sea salt, avocado, and lime juice. Using a potato masher or fork, mash the avocado and chickpeas together until you have a thick filling. Try not to mash the chickpeas all the way, as they create texture.Stir the celery and green onion into the filling and prepare yoursandwiches.

Layout two slices of bread, top them with the chickpea filling, some lettuce, and sliced tomato. Top them off with the two remainingslices, slice the sandwiches in half, and serve. Nutrition: Calories 471

89. **Pizza Bites**

Preparation Time: 1 Hour Cooking Time: 30 Minutes
Servings: 4
Ingredients:

Olive Oil (1 t.)

Dried Oregano (1 t.) Lemon Juice (1 t.) Dried Basil (1 t.)
Tomato Sauce (1 C.)Cauliflower (1 Head)Salt (to Taste)
Nutritional Yeast (to Taste) Garlic Cloves (2, Minced)
Directions:

Begin by prepping the oven to 300 and line a pan with parchment paper. When this is set, take a mixing bowl and combine the olive oil, oregano, basil, salt, tomato sauce, and the basil together. In a second bowl, you will want to place your nutritional yeast.

When you are ready, gently dip the cauliflower pieces into the tomatosauce and then roll in the nutritional yeast. You will want to place these on the baking sheet and continue until all of the cauliflower is covered.

Once the cauliflower is set, place it into the oven for about an hour oruntil the edges are crispy. Once they are cooked to your liking, remove from the oven and enjoy with some extra sauce for dipping!

Nutrition: Calories: 110 Proteins: 5g Carbs: 17g Fats: 3g

90. **Avocado, Spinach and Kale Soup**

Preparation time: 10 minutes Cooking time: 0 minutes
Servings: 4
Ingredients:

1 avocados, pitted, peeled and cut in halves 4 cups vegetable stock
2 tablespoons cilantro, chopped

Juice of 1 lime

1 teaspoon rosemary, dried

½ cup spinach leaves

½ cup kale, torn

Salt and black pepper to the tasteDirections:
In a blender, combine the avocados with the stock and the other ingredients, pulse well, divide into bowls and serve for lunch.

Nutrition: calories 300, fat 23, fiber 5, carbs 6, protein 7

91. Curry spinach soup

Preparation: 10 minutesCooking: 0 minutes Servings: 4

Ingredients:

1 cup almond milk

1 tablespoon green curry paste1 pound spinach leaves
1 tablespoon cilantro, chopped

Salt and black pepper to the taste4 cups veggie stock

2 tablespoon cilantro, choppedDirections:

In your blender, combine the almond milk with the curry paste and the other ingredients, pulse well, divide into bowls and serve for lunch. Nutrition: calories 240, fat 4, fiber 2, carbs 6, protein 2

92. Hot roasted peppers cream

Preparation: 10 minutes Cooking: 30 minutesServings: 4
Ingredients:

1 red chili pepper, minced4 garlic cloves, minced

2 pounds mixed bell peppers, roasted, peeled and chopped 4 scallions, chopped1 cup coconut cream
Salt and black pepper to the taste2 tablespoons olive oil
½ tablespoon basil, chopped4 cups vegetable stock
¼ cup chives, chopped

Directions:

Heat up a pot with the oil over medium heat, add the garlic and thechili pepper and sauté for 5 minutes.

Add the peppers and the other ingredients, toss, bring to a simmerand cook over medium heat for 25 minutes.

Blend the soup using an immersion blender, divide into bowls andserve.

Nutrition: calories 140, fat 2, fiber 2, carbs 5, protein 8

Recipes For Main Courses And Single Dishes

93. Smoked Tempeh with Broccoli Fritters

Preparation Time: 25 minutes Cooking Time: 20 minutes
Servings: 4
Ingredients:

For the flax egg:

4 tbsp flax seed powder + 12 tbsp water For the grilled tempeh:
3 tbsp olive oil

1 tbsp soy sauce

3 tbsp fresh lime juice 1 tbsp grated ginger
Salt and cayenne pepper to taste 10 oz. tempeh slices
For the broccoli fritters:

2 cups of rice broccoli8 oz. tofu cheese

3 tbsp plain flour

½ tsp onion powder1 tsp salt

¼ tsp freshly ground black pepper4¼ oz. vegan butter

For serving:

½ cup mixed salad greens1 cup vegan mayonnaise

½ lemon, juicedDirections:

For the smoked tempeh:

In a bowl, mix the flax seed powder with water and set aside to soak for 5 minutes.In another bowl, combine the olive oil, soy sauce, lime juice, grated ginger, salt, and cayenne pepper. Brush the tempeh slices with the mixture.

Heat a grill pan over medium heat and grill the tempeh on both sides until nicely smoked and golden brown, 8 minutes. Transfer to a plateand set aside in a warmer for serving.

In a medium bowl, combine the broccoli rice, tofu cheese, flour, onion, salt, and black pepper. Mix in the flax egg until well combine and form 1-inch thick patties out of the mixture.

Melt the vegan butter in a medium skillet over medium heat and fry the patties on both sides until golden brown, 8 minutes. Remove the fritters onto a plate and set aside.

In a small bowl, mix the vegan mayonnaise with the lemon juice.

Divide the smoked tempeh and broccoli fritters onto serving plates, add the salad greens, and serve with the vegan mayonnaise sauce.

94. Cheesy Potato Casserole

Preparation Time: 30 minutes Cooking Time: 20 minutes
Servings: 4
Ingredients:

2 oz. vegan butter

½ cup celery stalks, finely chopped 1 white onion, finely chopped

1 green bell pepper, seeded and finely chopped Salt and black pepper to taste

2 cups peeled and chopped potatoes 1 cup vegan mayonnaise

4 oz. freshly shredded vegan Parmesan cheese 1 tsp red chili flakes

Directions:

Preheat the oven to 400 F and grease a baking dish with cookingspray.

Season the celery, onion, and bell pepper with salt and blackpepper.

In a bowl, mix the potatoes, vegan mayonnaise, Parmesan cheese,and red chili flakes.

Pour the mixture into the baking dish, add the season vegetables,and mix well.

Bake in the oven until golden brown, about 20 minutes. Remove the baked potato and serve warm with baby spinach.

95. **Curry Mushroom Pie**

Preparation Time: 65 minutes Cooking Time: 1 hour
Servings: 4
Ingredients:

For the piecrust:

1 tbsp flax seed powder + 3 tbsp water

¾ cup plain flour 4 tbsp. chia seeds
4 tbsp almond flour

1 tbsp nutritional yeast1 tsp baking powder
1 pinch salt

3 tbsp olive oil4 tbsp water For the filling:
1 cup chopped baby Bella mushrooms 1 cup vegan mayonnaise

4 tbsp + 9 tbsp water

½ red bell pepper, finely chopped1 tsp curry powder
½ tsp paprika powder ½ tsp garlic powder

¼ tsp black pepper ½ cup coconut cream

1¼ cups shredded vegan Parmesan cheeseDirections:
In two separate bowls, mix the different portions of flaxseed powder with the respective quantity of water. Allow soaking for 5 minutes.

For the piecrust:

Preheat the oven to 350 F.

When the flax egg is ready, pour the smaller quantity into a food processor and pour in all the ingredients for the piecrust. Blend until soft, smooth dough forms.

Line an 8-inch springform pan with parchment paper and grease withcooking spray.

Spread the dough in the bottom of the pan and bake for 15 minutes.For the filling:
In a bowl, add the remaining flax egg and all the filling's ingredients.Combine well and pour the mixture on the piecrust. Bake further for 40 minutes or until the pie is golden brown.

Remove from the oven and allow cooling for 1 minute. Slice and serve the pie warm.

Nutrient-Packed Protein Salads

96. Arugula Lentil Salad

Preparation time: 5 mins. Cooking time: 5 mins.

Ingredient: ¾ cups cashews (¾ cups = 100 g) 1 onion
3 tbsp olive oil

1 chilli / jalapeño

5-6 sun-dried tomatoes in oil 3 slices bread (whole wheat)

1 cup brown lentils, cooked (1 cup = 1 / 15oz / 400 g)

1 handful arugula/rocket (1 handful = 100 g) 1-2 tbsp balsamic vinegar

salt and pepper to taste.

Directions:

Roast the cashews on a low heat for about three minutes

in a pan to maximize aroma. Then throw them into the salad bowl. Dice up and fry the onion in one third of the olive oil for about 3 minutes on a low heat. Meanwhile chop the chilli/jalapeño and dried tomatoes. Add them to the pan and fry for another 1-2 minutes. Cut the bread into big croutons. Move the onion mix into a big bowl. Now add the rest of the oil to the pan and fry the chopped-up bread until crunchy. Season with salt and pepper. Wash the arugula and add it to the bowl. Put the lentils in too, and mix them all around. Season with salt, pepper and balsamic vinegar. Serve with the croutons. Super tasty!

Flavour Boosters (Fish Glazes, Meat Rubs & Fish Rubs)

97. Tunisian Mixed Spiced Rub

This incredible rub recipe hailed from the Tunisian cooking secrets; the rub is the essential seasoning base for variety of Tunisian dishes.

This lovely spice blend created by caraway seeds, coriander, and hot pepper works like a charm on your favorite pork tenderloin, chicken as well as salmon.

Preparation Time: 5 min.Cooking Time: 5 min.

Servings: 5-½ tsp.Ingredients:

Coriander seeds - 2 tsp. Caraway seeds - 2 tsp. Crushed red pepper - 3/4 tsp.Garlic powder - 3/4 tsp.

Kosher salt - 1/2 tsp.Directions:

Mix in the coriander seeds, red pepper and caraway seeds

in your spice blender, grinder or processor to make this rub. Start processing or blending the mixed spices on "pulse" mode mixture to ground.

Put the mixed spice mixture into a bowl; mix in the salt and garlic powder. Mix again well.

Now, take your choice of meat cut and place it on a firm surface. Brush or rub the freshly made rub on it; pat gently for the rub to stick onto the surface. Turn the meat cut and repeat to spice up its other side. Repeat with other meat cuts.

The freshly rubbed meat is ready to be grilled or cooked!

98. All Purpose Dill Seed Rub

Boost your steak with vibrant, spiced flavors of this all-purpose dill seed rub. It also beautifully seasons chicken and pork meat cuts. Apply this unique rub minutes before grilling or cooking; you can also store it at room temperature for 12-14 days without sacrificing on its quality.

Preparation Time: 5 min.Cooking Time: 5 min.

Servings: 6-7 tsp.

Ingredients:

Paprika - 2 tsp.

Ground coriander - 2 tsp.Dill seed – 1 tsp.
Dry mustard - ½ tsp. Garlic, minced – 1 clove
Black pepper and salt as requiredCayenne pepper - ¼ tsp.
Directions:

Mix in all the rub ingredients in your mixing bowl to make the dillseed rub. Gently mix all ingredients using spatula or spoon to forman aromatic rub mixture.

Now, take your choice of meat cut and place it on a firm surface. Brush the freshly made rub on it; pat gently for the rub to stick onto the surface. Turn the meat cut and repeat to spice up its other side. Repeat with other meat cuts.

Let your meat cuts adequately season for more rich flavors for a few hours in your refrigerator. Take them out, as they are ready to be cooked or grilled!

Sauce Recipes

99. Vegan Ranch Dressing (Dipping Sauce)

Preparation time: 5 minutes Cooking time: 5 minutes
Servings: 8
Ingredients:

2 tablespoons lemon juice14 oz. silken tofu
1 tablespoon yellow mustard

1 tablespoon apple cider vinegar1 teaspoon onion granules
1 tablespoon agave

1 teaspoon garlic granules

2 tablespoons parsley, minced2 tablespoons dill, minced
1/2 teaspoon Himalayan salt

Directions:

Add all ingredients except parsley and dill to a blender

and blenduntil smooth at high speed.

Add dill and parsley and blend until mixed.Serve chilled.

100. Vegan Smokey Maple BBQ Sauce

Preparation time: 5 minutes Cooking time: 5 minutes Servings: 8
Ingredients:

1 tablespoon maple syrup1/2 cup ketchup
1 teaspoon garlic powder 1 teaspoon liquid smoke
Directions:

Add all ingredients to a bowl. Mix them until well combined.Serve and enjoy.

The Complete Plant Based Diet Cookbook

Healthy and Delicious Recipes to Lose Weight Feel Great on a Budget

Frank Smith

Breakfasts

101.   Oatmeal Fruit Shake

Preparation Time: 10 minutes Cooking time: 0 minutes
Servings: 2
Ingredients:

1 cup oatmeal, already prepared, cooled 1 apple, cored, roughly chopped
1 banana, halved

1 cup baby spinach 2 cups coconut water 2 cups ice, cubed
½ tsp ground cinnamon 1 tsp pure vanilla extract
Directions:
Add all ingredients to a blender.

Blend from low to high for several minutes until smooth.

Nutrition: Calories 270 Carbohydrates 58 g Fats 1.5 g
Protein 5 g

102. Amaranth Banana Breakfast Porridge

Preparation Time: 10 minutes Cooking time: 25 minutes
Servings: 8
Ingredients:

2 cup amaranth

2 cinnamon sticks

4 bananas, diced

2 Tbsp chopped pecans4 cups water
Directions:

Combine the amaranth, water, and cinnamon sticks, and banana in apot. Cover and let simmer around 25 minutes.

Remove from heat and discard the cinnamon. Places into bowls, andtop with pecans.

Nutrition: Calories 330 Carbohydrates 62 g Fats 6 g Protein 10 g

103. **Green Ginger Smoothie**

Preparation time: 5 minutes Cooking time: 5 minutes Servings: 2
Ingredients:

1 banana

½ apple sliced

1 orange sliced and peeled1 lemon juice
2 big spinach

1 tbsp. fresh ginger

½ cup almond milk

For the dressing: chia seeds, apple, raspberriesDirections:
Take a blender. Peel off and slice all fruits. Add banana, apple, orange, lime juice, ginger and spinach and blend them well until they turn smooth. Now add almond milk and pulse again for a few seconds. Pour the smoothie into glasses and serve. You can add chia seeds, apple or raspberries for a smoothie bowl. Store it up to 8-10 hours in the refrigerator.

Nutrition: Calories 330 Carbohydrates 62 g Fats 6 g Protein 10 g

104. Chocolate Strawberry Almond Protein Smoothie

Preparation time: 10 mCooking time: 10 m Ingredients:
1 cup of organic strawberries

1 1/2 cup homemade almond milk 1 scoop chocolate protein powder1 tablespoon organic coconut oil 1/4 cup organic raw almonds

1 tablespoon organic hemp seeds 1 tablespoon organic maca powderFor Garnish:

organic cacao nibs organic hemp seedsDirections:

Put all the ingredients inside a blender and beat until they are wellcombined.

Optional: Garnish with organic hemp seeds or organic cocoa beans.Enjoy it!

Nutrition: carbohydrates: 39 g calories: 720 Fat: 45 g sodium: 732g

protein: 44 g sugar: 12g

105.   Apple and Cinnamon Oatmeal

Preparation time: 10 minutes Cooking time:10 minutes Servings: 2

Ingredients

1¼ cups apple cider

1 apple, peeled, cored, and chopped

⅔ Cup rolled oats

1 teaspoon ground cinnamon

1 tablespoon pure maple syrup or agave (optional)

Directions

In a medium saucepan, bring the apple cider to a boil over medium-

high heat. Stir in the apple, oats, and cinnamon.

Bring the cereal to a boil and turn down heat to low. Simmer until the oatmeal thickens, 3 to 4 minutes. Spoon into two bowls and sweeten with maple syrup, if using. Serve hot.

106.   13 bis. Mango Key Lime Pie Smoothie

Preparation time: 5 minutes Cooking time: 0 minutes
Servings: 1
Ingredients

¼ Avocado 1 cup baby spinach

½ Cup frozen mango chunks

1 cup unsweetened soy or almond milk Juice of 1 lime (preferably a key lime). 1 tablespoon maple syrup
Directions

Combine all the Ingredients in a blender and blend until smooth.Enjoy immediately.

107. Spiced Orange Breakfast Couscous

Preparation time: 10 minutes Cooking time: 10 minutes Servings: 4

Ingredients

3 cups orange juice1½ cups couscous

1 teaspoon ground cinnamon

¼ Teaspoon ground cloves

½ Cup dried fruit, such as raisins or apricots

½ Cup chopped almonds or other nuts or seedsDirections In a small saucepan, bring the orange juice to a boil. Add the couscous, cinnamon, and cloves and remove from heat. Cover the pan with a lid and allow to sit until the couscous softens, about 5 minutes.

Fluff the couscous with a fork and stir in the dried fruit and nuts. Serve immediately.

108.   **Fig & Cheese Oatmeal**

Preparation Time: 10 minutes Cooking Time: 0 minute
Servings: 1
Ingredients:

½ cup water

½ cup rolled oatsPinch salt
2 tablespoons dried figs, sliced

2 tablespoons ricotta cheese

2 teaspoons agave syrup

1 tablespoon almonds, toasted and slicedDirections:
Put the water, oats and salt in a glass jar with lid.Shake to
blend well.
Refrigerate for up to 5 days.

Top with the remaining ingredients when ready to serve.

Nutrition: Calories: 294 Total fat: 8.5g Saturated fat: 2.3g
Cholesterol: 10mg Sodium: 182mg Potassium: 362mg
Carbohydrates: 47.5g Fiber: 6.6g Sugar: 16g Protein: 10.4g

109.   **Pumpkin Oats**

Preparation: 10 minutesCooking: 0 minute Servings: 1
Ingredients:

½ cup rolle oats ½ cup almond milk ¼ cup ricotta cheese

2 tablespoons pumpkin puree1 tablespoon maple syrup ¼ teaspoon vanilla 1/8 teaspoon ground nutmeg Directions:
Combine all the ingredients in a glass jar with lid.

Refrigerate for up to 5 days. Nutrition: Calories: 344 Total fat: 10g Saturated fat: 3.8g Cholesterol: 19mg Sodium: 179mg Potassium: 364mg Carbohydrates: 51.7g Fiber: 5.7g Sugar: 16g Protein: 13.3g

110.   **Apple Chia Pudding**

Preparation time: 10 minutes Cooking time: 5 minutes Servings: 04
Ingredients:

Chia Pudding:

4 tablespoons chia seeds1 cup almond milk
½ teaspoon cinnamonApple Pie Filling:
1 large apple, peeled, cored and chopped

¼ cup water

2 teaspoons maple syrupPinch cinnamon
2 tablespoons golden raisinsDirections:
In a sealable container, add cinnamon, chia seeds and almond milk,

mix well.

Seal the container and refrigerate overnight.

In a medium pot, combine all apple pie filling ingredients and cookfor 5 minutes.

Serve the chia pudding with apple filling on top.Enjoy.
Nutrition: Calories387TotalFat5.8gSaturatedFat4.2   g

Cholesterol 41 mg Sodium 154 mg Total Carbs 24.1 g Fiber 2.9 g

Sugar 3.1 g Protein 6.6 g

Soups, Salads, and Sides

111.   Garden
PatchSandwichesonMultigrain Bread

Preparation time: 15 minutes Cooking time: 0 minutes
Servings: 4 sandwiches Ingredients:

1pound extra-firm tofu, drained and patted dry1 medium red bell pepper, finely chopped

1 celery rib, finely chopped

3 green onions, minced

¼ cup shelled sunflower seeds

½ cup vegan mayonnaise, homemade or store-bought

½ teaspoon salt

½ teaspoon celery salt

¼ teaspoon freshly ground black pepper8 slices whole grain

bread

4 (¼-inch) slices ripe tomato

4 lettuce leavesDirections:

Crumble the tofu and place it in a large bowl. Add the bell pepper, celery, green onions, and sunflower seeds. Stir in the mayonnaise, salt, celery salt, and pepper and mix until well combined.

Toast the bread, if desired. Spread the mixture evenly onto 4 slices of the bread. Top each with a tomato slice, lettuce leaf, and the remaining bread. Cut the sandwiches diagonally in half and serve.

112.   **Garden Salad Wraps**

Preparation time: 15 minutes Cooking time: 10 minutes Servings: 4 wraps Ingredients:

6 tablespoons olive oil

2-pound extra-firm tofu, drained, patted dry, and cut into ½-inchstrips

1 tablespoon soy sauce

¼ cup apple cider vinegar

1 teaspoon yellow or spicy brown mustard

½ teaspoon salt

¼ teaspoon freshly ground black pepper 3 cups shredded romaine lettuce

3 ripe roma tomatoes, finely chopped

1 large carrot, shredded

1 medium english cucumber, peeled and chopped

⅓ cup minced red onion

¼ cup sliced pitted green olives

4 (10-inch) whole-grain flour tortillas or lavash flatbread Directions:

In a large skillet, heat 2 tablespoons of the oil over medium heat. Add the tofu and cook until golden brown, about 10 minutes. Sprinkle with soy sauce and set aside to cool.

In a small bowl, combine the vinegar, mustard, salt, and pepper with the remaining 4 tablespoons oil, stirring to blend well. Set aside.

In a large bowl, combine the lettuce, tomatoes, carrot, cucumber, onion, and olives. Pour on the dressing and toss to coat.

To assemble wraps, place 1 tortilla on a work surface and spread with about one-quarter of the salad. Place a few strips of tofu on the tortilla and roll up tightly. Slice in half

113.   **Marinated Mushroom Wraps**

Preparation time: 15 minutes Cooking time: 0 minutes Servings: 2 wraps Ingredients:

3 tablespoons soy sauce

3 tablespoons fresh lemon juice

1¹/2 tablespoons toasted sesame oil

2 portobello mushroom caps, cut into ¼-inch strips 1 ripe hass avocado, pitted and peeled
2 cups fresh baby spinach leaves

1 medium red bell pepper, cut into ¼-inch strips 1 ripe tomato, chopped
Salt and freshly ground black pepper

Directions:

In a medium bowl, combine the soy sauce, 2 tablespoons of the lemon juice, and the oil. Add the portobello strips, toss to combine, and marinate for 1 hour or overnight. Drain the mushrooms and set aside.

Mash the avocado with the remaining 1 tablespoon of lemon juice.

To assemble wraps, place 1 tortilla on a work surface and spread with some of the mashed avocado. Top with a layer of baby spinach leaves. In the lower third of each tortilla, arrange strips of the soakedmushrooms and some of the bell pepper strips. Sprinkle with the tomato and salt and black pepper to taste. Roll up tightly and cut in half diagonally. Repeat with the remaining ingredients and serve.

Entrées

114.   Homemade Trail Mix

Preparation time: 20 minutes Cooking time: 20 minutes
Servings: 2
Ingredients:

½ cup uncooked old-fashioned oatmeal

½ cup chopped dates

2 cups whole grain cereal

¼ cup raisins

¼ cup almonds

¼ cup walnutsDirections:
Mix all the ingredients in a large bowl.

Place in an airtight container until ready to use.

115.   Nut Butter Maple Dip

Preparation time: 1 hourCooking time: 1 hour Servings:
Ingredients:

½ tablespoon ground flaxseed 1 teaspoon ground
cinnamon
½ tablespoon maple syrup

2 tablespoons cashew milk

¾ cups crunchy, unsweetened peanut butterDirections:
In a bowl, combine the flaxseed, cinnamon, maple
syrup, cashew

milk and peanut butter.

Use a fork to mix everything in. I stir it like I'm
scrambling eggs. Themixture should be creamy. If it's too
runny, add a little more peanut butter; if it's too thick, add
a little more cashew milk.

Refrigerate for about an hour, covered and serve.

Smoothies and Beverages

116.   Kale & Avocado Smoothie

Preparation Time: 10 Minutes Cooking time: 0 minute
Servings: 1
Ingredients:

1 ripe banana

1 cup kale

1 cup almond milk

¼ avocado

1 tbsp. chia seeds2 tsp. honey
1 cup ice cubes

Direction:

Blend all the ingredients until smooth.

Nutrition: Calories 343 Total Fat 14 gSaturated Fat 2

g Cholesterol 0 mgSodium 199 mgTotal Carbohydrate 55 g Dietary Fiber 12 g Protein 6 gTotal Sugars 29 gPotassium 1051mg

117.   Coconut & Strawberry Smoothie

Preparation Time: 10 Minutes Cooking Time: 0 minutes
Serves: 1
Calories: 278

Protein: 14 Grams

Fat: 2 Grams

Carbs: 57 GramsIngredients:
1 Cup Strawberries, Frozen & Thawed Slightly

1 Ripe Banana, Sliced & Frozen

½ Cup Coconut Milk, Light

½ Cup Vegan Yogurt

1 Tablespoon Chia Seeds

1 Teaspoon Lime juice, Fresh4 Ice Cubes
Directions:

Blend everything together until smooth, and serve immediately.

118.   Pumpkin Chia Smoothie

Preparation Time: 5 Minutes Cooking Time: 0 minutes
Serves: 1
Calories: 726

Protein: 5.5 Grams

Fat: 69.8 Grams

Carbs: 15 GramsIngredients:
3 Tablespoons Pumpkin Puree

1 Tablespoon MCT Oil

¾ Cup Coconut Milk, Full Fat

½ Avocado, Fresh

1 Teaspoon Vanilla, Pure

½ Teaspoon Pumpkin Pie SpiceDirections:
Combine all ingredients together until blended.

119.　　**Mini Berry Tarts**

Preparation Time: 35 minutes + 1 hour chillingServings: 4
Tickle-sized berries-filled with surprises, oh so delicious! Also so delicious that you can't stop having them.

Ingredients

For the piecrust:

4 tbsp flax seed powder + 12 tbsp water

1/3 cup whole-wheat flour + more for dusting

½ tsp salt

¼ cup plant butter, cold and crumbled 3 tbsp pure malt syrup
1 ½ tsp vanilla extractFor the filling:
6 oz cashew cream

6 tbsp pure date sugar

¾ tsp vanilla extract

1 cup mixed frozen berriesDirections
Preheat the oven to 350 F and grease a mini pie pans with cooking

spray.

In a medium bowl, mix the flax seed powder with water and allowsoaking for 5 minutes.

In a large bowl, combine the flour and salt. Add the

butter and using an electric hand mixer, whisk until crumbly. Pour in the flax egg, malt

syrup, vanilla, and mix until smooth dough forms.

Flatten the dough on a flat surface, cover with plastic wrap, and refrigerate for 1 hour.

After, lightly dust a working surface with some flour, remove the dough onto the surface, and using a rolling pin, flatten the dough intoa 1-inch diameter circle,

Use a large cookie cutter, cut out rounds of the dough and fit into the pie pans. Use a knife to trim the edges of the pan. Lay a parchment paper on the dough cups, pour on some baking beans and bake in the oven until golden brown, 15 to 20 minutes.

Remove the pans from the oven, pour out the baking beans, and allow cooling.

In a medium bowl, mix the cashew cream, date sugar, and vanilla extract.

Divide the mixture into the tart cups and top with berries. Serve immediately.

Nutritional info per serving

Calories 545 | Fats 33.5g| Carbs 53.6g | Protein 10.6g

120.   **Mixed Nut Chocolate Fudge**

Preparation Time: 2 hours 10 minutes

Servings: 4

A recipe for chocolate fudge that takes just 10 minutes to make andrequires ingredients that are readily available.

Ingredients

3 cups unsweetened chocolate chips

¼ cup thick coconut milk

1 ½ tsp vanilla extractA pinch salt
1 cup chopped mixed nuts

Directions

Line a 9-inch square pan with baking paper and set aside.

Melt the chocolate chips, coconut milk, and vanilla in a medium potover low heat.

Mix in the salt and nuts until well distributed and pour the mixtureinto the square pan.

Refrigerate for at least for at least 2 hours.

Remove from the fridge, cut into squares and serve.
Nutritional info per serving
Calories 907 | Fats 31.5g| Carbs 152.1g | Protein 7.7g

121.   **Date Cake Slices**

Preparation Time: 1 hour 20 minutes

Servings: 4

With a slightly thick yet fluffy texture, they're super soft.
Ingredients
½ cup cold plant butter, cut in pieces, plus extra for greasing1 tbsp flax seed powder + 3 tbsp water
½ cup whole-wheat flour, plus extra for dusting

¼ cup chopped pecans and walnuts1 tsp baking powder
1 tsp baking soda

1 tsp cinnamon powder

1 tsp salt

1/3 cup water

1/3 cup pitted dates, chopped

½ cup pure date sugar1 tsp vanilla extract
¼ cup pure date syrup for drizzling.

Directions

Preheat the oven to 350 F and lightly grease a round baking dishwith some plant butter.

In a small bowl, mix the flax seed powder with water and allow thickening for 5 minutes to make the flax egg.

In a food processor, add the flour, nuts, baking powder, baking soda, cinnamon powder, and salt. Blend until well combined.

Add the water, dates, date sugar, and vanilla. Process until smooth with tiny pieces of dates evident.

Pour the batter into the baking dish and bake in the oven for 1 hour and 10 minutes or until a toothpick inserted comes out clean. Remove the dish from the oven, invert the cake onto a serving platter to cool, drizzle with the date syrup, slice, and serve.

Nutritional info per serving

Calories 850 | Fats 61.2g| Carbs 65.7g | Protein 12.8g

122.   Chocolate Mousse Cake

Preparation Time: 40 minutes + 6 hours 30 minutes chillingServings: 4

Have a cake with a basic mousse of chocolate and tell me how youfeel.

Ingredients

2/3 cup toasted almond flour

¼ cup unsalted plant butter, melted

2 cups unsweetened chocolate bars, broken into pieces 2 ½ cups coconut cream

Fresh raspberries or strawberries for toppingDirections

Lightly grease a 9-inch springform pan with some plant butter andset aside.

Mix the almond flour and plant butter in a medium bowl and pour the mixture into the springform pan. Use the spoon to spread and press the mixture into the bottom of the pan. Place in the refrigerator to firm for 30 minutes.

Meanwhile, pour the chocolate in a safe microwave bowl and meltfor 1 minute stirring every 30 seconds.

Remove from the microwave and mix in the coconut cream and maple syrup.

Remove the cake pan from the oven, pour the chocolate mixture on top making to sure to shake the pan and even the layer. Chill further for 4 to 6 hours.

Take out the pan from the fridge, release the cake and garnish with the raspberries or strawberries.

Slice and serve. Nutritional info per serving

Calories 608 | Fats 60.5g| Carbs 19.8g | Protein 6.3g

Snacks and Desserts

123.   Nori Snack Rolls

Preparation Time: 5 minutes Cooking time: 10 minutes Servings: 4 rolls
Ingredients

2 tablespoons almond, cashew, peanut, or others nut butter2 tablespoons tamari, or soy sauce
4 standard nori sheets

1 mushroom, sliced

1 tablespoon pickled ginger

½ cup grated carrotsDirections
Preparing the Ingredients. Preheat the oven to 350°F.
Mix together the nut butter and tamari until smooth and very thick. Lay out a nori sheet, rough side up, the long way.

Spread a thin line of the tamari mixture on the far end of the nori sheet, from side to side. Lay the mushroom slices, ginger, and carrots in a line at the other end (the end closest to you).

Fold the vegetables inside the nori, rolling toward the tahini mixture, which will seal the roll. Repeat to make 4 rolls.

Put on a baking sheet and bake for 8 to 10 minutes, or until the rolls are slightly browned and crispy at the ends. Let the rolls cool for a few minutes, then slice each roll into 3 smaller pieces.

Nutrition: Calories: 79; Total fat: 5g; Carbs: 6g; Fiber: 2g; Protein: 4g

124.   **Risotto Bites**

Preparation Time: 15 minutes Cooking time: 20 minutes Servings: 12 bites Ingredients

½ cup panko bread crumbs1 teaspoon paprika

1 teaspoon chipotle powder or ground cayenne pepper

1½ cups cold Green Pea Risotto Nonstick cooking spray Directions

Preparing the Ingredients. Preheat the oven to 425°F.

Line a baking sheet with parchment paper.

On a large plate, combine the panko, paprika, and chipotle powder. Set aside.

Roll 2 tablespoons of the risotto into a ball.

Gently roll in the bread crumbs, and place on the prepared baking sheet. Repeat to make a total of 12 balls.

Spritz the tops of the risotto bites with nonstick cooking spray and bake for 15 to 20 minutes, until they begin to brown. Cool completely before storing in a large airtight container in a single layer (add a piece of parchment paper for a second layer) or in a plastic freezer bag.

Nutrition: Calories: 100; Fat: 2g; Protein: 6g; Carbohydrates: 17g;Fiber: 5g; Sugar: 2g; Sodium: 165 mg

125. Jicama and Guacamole

Preparation Time: 15 minutes Cooking time: 0 minutes
Servings: 4
Ingredients

juice of 1 lime, or 1 tablespoon prepared lime juice

2 hass avocados, peeled, pits removed, and cut into cubes

½ teaspoon sea salt

½ red onion, minced 1 garlic clove, minced
¼ cup chopped cilantro (optional)

1 jicama bulb, peeled and cut into matchsticksDirections
Preparing the Ingredients.

In a medium bowl, squeeze the lime juice over the top of theavocado and sprinkle with salt.

Lightly mash the avocado with a fork. Stir in the onion, garlic, andcilantro, if using.

Serve with slices of jicama to dip in guacamole.

To store, place plastic wrap over the bowl of guacamole andrefrigerate. The guacamole will keep for about 2 days.

126.   Oven-baked   Caramelize Plantains

Preparation time: 30 minutes Cooking time: 17 minutes Servings: 4

Ingredients

4 medium plantains, peeled and sliced2 Tbsp fresh orange juice

4 Tbsp brown sugar or to taste

1 Tbsp grated orange zest

4 Tbsp coconut butter, meltedDirections
Preheat oven to 360 F/180 C.

Place plantain slices in a heatproof dish.

Pour the orange juice over plantains, and then sprinkle with brownsugar and grated orange zest.

Melt coconut butter and pour evenly over plantains.Cover with foil and bake for 15 to 17 minutes.

Serve warm or cold with honey or maple syrup.

127.   **Powerful Peas & Lentils Dip**

Preparation time: 10 minutes Cooking time: 0 minutes
Servings: 4
Ingredients

4 cups frozen peas

2 cup green lentils cooked 1 piece of grated ginger
1/2 cup fresh basil chopped 1 cup ground almonds Juice
of 1/2 lime
Pinch of salt

4 Tbsp sesame oil

1/4 cup Sesame seeds Directions
Place all ingredients in a food processor or in a blender.

Blend until all ingredients combined well.

Keep refrigerated in an airtight container up to 4 days.

128.   Protein "Raffaello" Candies

Preparation time: 15 minutes Cooking time: 0 minutes
Servings: 12
Ingredients

1 1/2 cups desiccated coconut flakes 1/2 cup coconut butter softened
4 Tbsp coconut milk canned

4 Tbs coconut palm sugar (or granulated sugar)1 tsp pure vanilla extract1 Tbsp vegan protein powder (pea or soy)15 whole almonds
Directions

Put 1 cup of desiccated coconut flakes, and all remaining ingredients in the blender (except almonds), and blend until soft.

If your dough is too thick, add some coconut milk. In a bowl, add remaining coconut flakes.
Coat every almond in one tablespoon of mixture and roll into a ball.Roll each ball in coconut flakes.
Chill in the fridge for several hours.

129.   **Roasted Cauliflower**

Preparation Time: 30 Minutes Cooking Time: 20 Minutes
Servings: 4
Ingredients:

Olive Oil (1 T.) Cauliflower (1, Chopped)Salt (to Taste)

Smoked Paprika (2 t.)Parsley (2 T.) Directions:

If you like to snack, it is better to have healthier
options at hand. You'll want to start this recipe off by
prepping your oven to 450.

As this warms up, place the cauliflower florets into a large
mixing bowl and toss with the olive oil, salt, and smoked
paprika. Once this is complete, lay it across a baking sheet
and pop it into the oven for 20 minutes.

When the cauliflower is cooked to your liking, remove
from the oven,top with parsley, and you are all set.

Nutrition: Calories: 70 Proteins: 3g Carbs: 8g Fats: 5g

Dinner Recipes

130. Cauliflower Steak Kicking Corn

Preparation: 30 min.Cooking: 60 min.Servings: 6

Ingredients:

2 t. capers, drained 4 scallions, chopped1 red chili, minced ¼ c. vegetable oil

2 ears of corn, shucked 2 big cauliflower heads Salt and pepper to tasteDirections:
Heat the oven to 375 degrees.

Boil a pot of water, about 4 cups, using the maximum heat setting available.

Add corn in the saucepan, cooking approximately 3 minutes or untiltender.

Drain and allow the corn to cool, then slice the kernels away from thecob.

Warm 2 tablespoons of vegetable oil in a skillet.

Combine the chili pepper with the oil, cooking for approximately 30seconds.

Next, combine the scallions, sautéing with the chili pepper until soft. Mix in the corn and capers in the skillet and cook for approximately 1 minute to blend the flavors. Then remove from heat. Warm 1 tablespoon of vegetable oil in a skillet. Once warm, begin to place cauliflower steaks to the pan, 2 to 3 at a time. Season to your liking with salt and cook over medium heat for 3 minutes or until lightly browned. Once cooked, slide onto the cookie sheet and repeat step 5 with the remaining cauliflower.

Take the corn mixture and press into the spaces between the florets of the cauliflower.

Bake for 25 minutes. Serve warm and enjoy!
Nutrition: Calories: 153 | Carbohydrates: 15 g | Proteins: 4 g | Fats:10 g

131.   Green beans stir fry

Preparation time 30 minutes

Cooking time: 10 minutesServings: 6-8 Ingredients:

1 1/2 pounds of green beans, stringed, chopped into 1 ½-inchpieces

1 large onion, thinly sliced4 star anise (optional)

3 tablespoons avocado oil

1 1/2 tablespoons tamari sauce or soy sauceSalt to taste 3/4 cup water

Direction:

Place a wok over medium heat. Add oil. When oil is heated, addonions and sauté until onions are translucent.

Add beans, water, tamari sauce, and star anise and stir. Cover andcook until the beans are tender.

Uncover, add salt and raise the heat to high. Cook until the waterdries up in the wok. Stir a couple of times while cooking.

132.   **Mean bean minestrone**

Preparation time: 45 minutes Cooking time: 40 minutes Servings: 6

Protein content per serving: 9gIngredients

1 tablespoon (15 ml) olive oil

1/3 cup (80 g) chopped red onion

4 cloves garlic, grated or pressed

1 leek, white and light green parts, trimmed and chopped (about 4ounces, or 113 g)

2 carrots, peeled and minced (about 4 ounces, or 113 g)2 ribs of celery, minced (about 2 ounces, or 57 g)

2 yellow squashes, trimmed and chopped (about 8 ounces, or 227 g) 1 green bell pepper, trimmed and chopped (about 8 ounces, or 227 g)

1 tablespoon (16 g) tomato paste1 teaspoon dried oregano

1 teaspoon dried basil

⅓ teaspoon smoked paprika

'¼ To ¼ teaspoon cayenne pepper, or to taste

2 cans (each 15 ounces, or 425 g) diced fire-roasted tomatoes4 cups (940 ml) vegetable broth, more if needed

3 cups (532 g) cannellini beans, or other white beans

2 cups (330 g) cooked farro, or other whole grain or pasta Salt, to taste

Nut and seed sprinkles, for garnish, optional and to taste

Directions:

In a large pot, add the oil, onion, garlic, leek, carrots, celery, yellow

squash, bell pepper, tomato paste, oregano, basil, paprika, and cayenne pepper. Cook on medium-high heat, stirring often until the vegetables start to get tender, about 6 minutes.

Add the tomatoes and broth. Bring to a boil, lower the heat, cover with a lid, and simmer 15 minutes.

Add the beans and simmer another 10 minutes. Add the farro and simmer 5 more minutes to heat the farro.

Note that this is a thick minestrone. If there are leftovers (which tasteeven better, by the way), the soup will thicken more once chilled.

Add extra broth if you prefer a thinner soup and adjust seasoning if needed. Add nut and seed sprinkles on each portion upon serving, if desired.

Store leftovers in an airtight container in the refrigerator for up to 5 days. The minestrone can also be frozen for up to 3 months.

Lunch Recipes

133. Chickpea And Edamame Salad

Preparation Time: 40 minutes Cooking Time: 0 minutes
Serving: 4
Ingredients:

For the Salad:

3 tablespoons dried cranberries 1/4 cup (59 grams) diced carrots
3/4 cup (177 grams) edamame soybeans 1/3 cup (78 grams) chopped green pepper 30 ounces (850 grams) cooked chickpeas 1/3 cup (78 grams) chopped red pepper 1/2 teaspoon minced garlic
For the Dressing:

1/4 teaspoon dried oregano 1 teaspoon coconut sugar 1/4 teaspoon dried basil
1/3 teaspoon ground black pepper

1/3 teaspoon salt

1/4 teaspoon dried rosemary1 teaspoon white vinegar
2 tablespoons grape seed oil 2 tablespoons olive oil
Directions:
Preparethe salad: takealargesaladbowl, place allsalad ingredients in it and then toss until properly mixed.

Preparehe dressing:takeasmall bowl,placealldressing ingredients in it and then whisk until combined.

Drizzle dressing over salad and toss until well mixed.

Place the salad bowl in the refrigerator for at least 30 minutes untilchilled, then serve.

Nutrition: 119.6 Cal; 1.9 g Fat; 0.1 g Saturated Fat; 20.8 g Carbs; 4.8g Fiber; 6 g Protein; 1.1 g Sugar;

134.   Cauliflower Salad

Preparation Time: 20 minutes Cooking Time: 15 minutes
Servings: 4
Ingredients:

8 cups cauliflower florets

5 tablespoons olive oil, dividedSalt and pepper to taste
1 cup parsley

1 clove garlic, minced

2 tablespoons lemon juice

¼ cup almonds, toasted and sliced3 cups arugula
2 tablespoons olives, sliced

¼ cup feta, crumbledDirection
Preheat your oven to 425 degrees F.

Toss the cauliflower in a mixture of 1 tablespoon olive oil, salt andpepper.Place in a baking pan and roast for 15 minutes.Put the parsley, remaining oil, garlic, lemon juice, salt and pepper ina blender.Pulse until smooth.

Place the roasted cauliflower in a salad bowl.

Stir in the rest of the ingredients along with the parsley dressing.

Nutrition: Calories: 198 Total fat: 16.5g Saturated fat: 3g Cholesterol: 6mg Sodium: 3mg Potassium: 570mg

Carbohydrates: 10.4g Fiber: 4.1g Sugar: 4g Protein: 5.4g

135. Garlic Mashed Potatoes & Turnips

Preparation: 20 minutesCooking: 30 minutes Servings: 8
Ingredients:

1 head garlic 1 teaspoon olive oil lb. turnips, sliced into cubes lb. potatoes, sliced into cubes

½ cup almond milk

½ cup vegan parmesan cheese, grated 1 tablespoon fresh thyme, chopped

1 tablespoon fresh chives, chopped 2 tablespoons vegan butter

Salt and pepper to tasteDirection

Preheat your oven to 375 degrees F. Slice the tip off the garlic head.

Drizzle with a little oil and roast in the oven for 45 minutes.

Boil the turnips and potatoes in a pot of water for 30 minutes or untiltender.

Add all the ingredients to a food processor along with the garlic.Pulse until smooth.

Nutrition: Calories: 141 Total fat: 3.2g Saturated fat: 1.5g Cholesterol: 7mg Sodium: 284mg Potassium: 676mg Carbohydrates: 24.6g Fiber: 3.1g Sugar: 4g Protein: 4.6g

136.   Pulled "Pork" Sandwiches

This pulled "pork" is the perfect dish to make ahead. Prepare the mushrooms and coat them in the sauce and then you can store them chilled in the cold-storage box or the icebox. If you prepare a large amount to keep in the icebox, you will always have some on hand for sandwiches, pizza, nachos, or any other vegan-version of popular dishes that might be complemented by pulled "pork".

Preparation time: 40 minutes Cooking Time: 35 minutes
Servings: 3
Ingredients:

King oyster mushrooms* – 4 Barbecue sauce – .25 cup
Olive oil – 2 tablespoons Sea salt – .25 teaspoon Garlic, minced – 2 cloves
Cayenne pepper – .25 teaspoon Bread – 6 slices
Directions:

Start by setting your electric cooker to Fahrenheit 400 degrees.

While your electric cooker warms up, clean the mushrooms with a damp paper towel and then use two forks to shred both the caps and stems of the mushrooms into pieces resembling pulled pork. Place

the shredded mushrooms on a kitchen parchment-lined aluminum baking sheet.

Drizzle the mushrooms with half of the olive oil and then toss them with the seasoning and garlic until evenly coated. Allow the oyster mushrooms to roast until slightly crispy and browned about twenty minutes.

In a skillet, add the remaining tablespoon of olive oil, allowing it to warm over midway-elevated. Put the cooked mushrooms in the pan along with the barbecue sauce.

Cook the mushrooms in the sauce while stirring until the sauce is fragrant and warm, about three to five minutes. Top three slices of bread with this concoction and top with the remaining three slices. Cut the sandwiches in half before serving. Note:

*If you can't find king oyster mushrooms, then you can use three heaping cups of regular oyster mushrooms.

Nutrition: Calories 259

137. Coconut zucchini cream

Preparation time: 10 minutes Cooking time: 25 minutes
Servings: 4
Ingredients:

1 pound zucchinis, roughly chopped 2 tablespoons avocado oil
4 scallions, chopped

Salt and black pepper to the taste6 cups veggie stock
1 teaspoon basil, dried

1 teaspoon cumin, ground3 garlic cloves, minced
¾ cup coconut cream

1 tablespoon dill, choppedDirections:
Heat up a pot with the oil over medium high heat, add the scallions

and the garlic and sauté for 5 minutes.

Add the rest of the ingredients, stir, bring to a simmer and cook overmedium heat for 20 minutes more.

Blend the soup using an immersion blender, ladle into bowls andserve.

Nutrition: calories 160, fat 4, fiber 2, carbs 4, protein 8

138.   Zucchini and Cauliflower Soup

Preparation time: 10 minutesCooking time: 25 minutes

Servings: 4Ingredients:

4 scallions, chopped

1 teaspoon ginger, grated2 tablespoons olive oil

1 pound zucchinis, sliced

2 cups cauliflower florets

Salt and black pepper to the taste6 cups veggie stock
1 garlic clove, minced

1 tablespoon lemon juice1 cup coconut cream Directions:

Heat up a pot with the oil over medium heat, add the scallions,ginger and the garlic and sauté for 5 minutes.

Add the rest of the ingredients, bring to a simmer and cook overmedium heat for 20 minutes.

Blend everything using an immersion blender, ladle into soup bowlsand serve.

Nutrition: calories 154, fat 12, fiber 3, carbs 5, protein 4

139.   Chard soup

Preparation time: 10 minutes Cooking time: 25 minutes
Servings: 4
Ingredients:

1 pound Swiss chard, chopped

½ cup shallots, chopped 1 tablespoon avocado oil 1 teaspoon cumin, ground

1 teaspoon rosemary, dried1 teaspoon basil, dried

2 garlic cloves, minced

Salt and black pepper to the taste6 cups vegetable stock
1 tablespoon tomato passata

1 tablespoon cilantro, choppedDirections:
Heat up a pan with the oil over medium heat, add the shallots and

the garlic and sauté for 5 minutes.

Add the swiss chard and the other ingredients, toss, bring to a simmer and cook over medium heat for 20 minutes more.

Divide the soup into bowls and serve.

Nutrition: calories 232, fat 23, fiber 3, carbs 4, protein 3

140.   **Eggplant and Olives Stew**

Preparation time: 10 minutes Cooking time: 30 minutes
Servings: 4
Ingredients:

2 scallions, chopped

2 tablespoons avocado oil

2 garlic cloves, chopped 1 bunch parsley, chopped
Salt and black pepper to the taste

1 teaspoon basil, dried 1 teaspoon cumin, dried
2 eggplants, roughly cubed

1 cup green olives, pitted and sliced3 tablespoons balsamic vinegar
½ Cup tomato passataDirections:

Heat up a pot with the oil over medium heat, add the scallions, garlic,basil and cumin and sauté for 5 minutes.

Add the eggplants and the other ingredients, toss, cook over mediumheat for 25 minutes more, divide into bowls and serve.

Nutrition: calories 93, fat 1.8, fiber 10.6, carbs 18.6, protein 3.4

Recipes For Main Courses And Single Dishes

141. Pecan & Blueberry Crumble

Preparation Time: 40 Minutes Cooking Time: 1 Hour
Servings: 6
Calories: 381

Protein: 10 Grams

Fat: 32 Grams

Net Carbs: 20 GramsIngredients:
14 Ounces Blueberries

1 Tablespoon Lemon Juice, Fresh 1 ½ Teaspoon Stevia Powder
3 Tablespoons Chia Seeds

2 Cups Almond Flour, Blanched

¼ Cup Pecans, Chopped 5 Tablespoon coconut Oil 2 Tablespoon Cinnamon Directions:

Mix together your blueberries, stevia, chia seeds and lemon juice,and place it in an iron skillet.

Mix ingredients while spreading it over your blueberries.

Heat your oven to 400, and then transfer it to an oven safe skillet,baking for a half hour.

Interesting Facts: Blueberries: These guys are a delectable treat thatis easily incorporated into many dishes. They are packed with antioxidants and Vitamin C. Bonus: Blueberries have been proven to promote eye health and slow macular degeneration.

142. **Rice Pudding**

Preparation Time: 1 Hour 35 Minutes Cooking Time: 1 Hour and 30 MinutesServings: 6
Ingredients:

1 Cup Brown Rice

1 Teaspoon Vanilla Extract, Pure

½ Teaspoon Sea Salt, Fine

½ Teaspoon Cinnamon

¼ Teaspoon Nutmeg3 Egg Substitutes
3 Cups Coconut Milk, Light

2 Cups Brown Rice, CookedDirections:
Blend all of your ingredients together before pouring them into a twoquarter dish.

Bake at 300 for ninety minutes before serving.

Interesting Facts: Brown rice is incredibly high in antioxidants and good vitamins. It's relative, 14 white rice is far less beneficial as much of these healthy nutrients get destroyed during the process of milling. You can also opt for red and black rice or wild rice. The meal options for this healthy grain are limitless!

Nutrient-Packed Protein Salads

143.   Chickpea, Red Kidney Bean And Feta Salad

Preparation time: 5 minsCooking time: 5 mins Ingredient:

1 can chickpeas

1 can red kidney beans

1 piece small of ginger grated or shredded 1 medium onion diced
2- 3 cloves garlic

1   tbsp olive oil

A pinch of red chili flakes

3-4 spring onions green part only, chopped, scallions 1 cup chopped parsley OR coriander I used cilantro Juice of one lemon150 g feta cheese – almost half cup size Salt and Black pepper.

Directions:

Heat 1 tablespoon of olive oil and cook the onion till lightly golden.Do not overdo it and the onions should still be crunchy. Add garlic, ginger and chili and cook till the garlic is fragrant. Set aside to coolso it doesn't melt the feta when you mix it in. Drain the chickpeas and red kidney beans, rinse and place in the salad bowl. Add crumbled feta, spring onion, parsley (or coriander) and lemon juice, season with salt and pepper. Add the cooled onion and garlic mixtureand remaining oil and mix well.

144. Curried Carrot Slaw With Tempeh

Preparation: 10 minsCooking: 10 mins

Ingredient:

8 ounces tempeh, sliced into triangles1/4 tsp liquid smoke (optional) 1 1/2 Tbsp maple syrup, grade B

1 tsp extra virgin olive oil or virgin coconut oil2-3 tsp tamari or 2 tsp soy sauce

1 Tbsp crushed raw walnuts4 cups shredded carrots

1 small onion, diced 1 Tbsp curry powder

1/4 tsp turmeric powder (for added turmeric power, optional) 1/8 tsp black pepper2 Tbsp tahini

1/4 cup fresh lemon juice sweet stuff: 1 – 1 1/2 Tbsp maple syrup + an optional handful orraisins

1/2 cup flat leaf parsley, finely chopped + some for garnish

a few pinches of cayenne for heat (optional) salt and pepper for carrot salad – to taste.

Directions:

Warm a skillet up over high heat and add in the coconut or olive oil. When oil is hot, add the tempeh triangles, tamari, maple and liquid smoke. Flip the tempeh around a bit to allow it to absorb the liquid. Cook for about 5 minutes, flipping the tempeh a few times throughout the cooking process. When tempeh is browned and edges blackened a bit, and all liquid absorbed, turn off heat.

Sprinklethe walnut pieces and some black pepper over top the tempeh and set pan aside to keep triangles warm in skillet. In a large mixingbowl, add the carrots, tahini, lemon juice, spices, parsley, maple syrup, optional raisins and onion. Toss very well for a few minutes to marinate the carrots with the dressing. For a creamier salad, add another spoonful of tahini. To thin things out and make the salad zestier, add another splash of lemon juice or a teaspoon of apple cider vinegar. Finally, add salt and pepper to the carrot salad totaste. Pour the carrot salad in a large serving bowl and top with the tempeh. Serve right away or place in the fridge to serve in a few hours or up to a day later. The carrots will soften the longer they set in the fridge.

145.   Black & White Bean Quinoa Salad

Preparation time: 15 mins Cooking time: 15 mins
Ingredient:

⅓ cup (75 mL) quinoa

1 can (19 oz/540 mL) black beans, drained and rinsed

1 can (19 oz/540 mL) navy beans, drained and rinsed 1 cup (250 mL) diced cucumbers
¼ cup (50 mL) diced red onion

1 jalapeno pepper, seeded and minced (I've never used it and find the dish spicy enough for me, but feel free to add it if you like things hot!)

¼ cup (50 mL) chopped fresh coriander (cilantro)

¼ cup (50 mL) vegetable oil (I use cold pressed extra-virgin olive oil)

2 tbsp (25 mL) lime juice

1 tbsp (15 mL) cider vinegar 1 clove garlic, minced
½ tsp (2 mL) chili powder

1 tsp (5 mL) ground coriander

½ tsp (2 mL) dried oregano

¼ tsp (1 mL) salt

¼ tsp (1 mL) pepper.

Directions:

In saucepan of boiling salted ⅔ C water, cook quinoa until tender, about 12 minutes. Drain and rinse. Dressing: In large bowl, whisk together oil, lime juice, vinegar, garlic, chili powder, coriander, oregano, salt and pepper. Add quinoa, black beans, navy beans, cucumber, onion, jalapeño pepper and coriander; toss to combine.

146. Greek Salad With Seitan Gyros Strips

Preparation time: 5 mins

Cooking time: 5 minsIngredient: 4 tomatoes
1 punnet cherry tomatoes

1 1/2 crunchy cucumbers

1 big handful kalamata olives 1/2 Spanish onion finely sliced
1/4 stick of Cheesy mozzarella style cheese.Fresh oregano and mint
1/4 cup good quality extra virgin olive oil

2 Tablespoons vinegar (red wine or balsamic) 1 teaspoon castor sugar
2 teaspoons mixed dried Italian herbs 1 clove finely chopped garlic
2 teaspoon soy saucesalt
pepper.

Directions:

In a small frying pan, place gyros strips and fry until slightly blackened on the edges. Leave to cool. Cut up all your veggies roughly and place in a large bowl. Add olives, oregano, mint and chopped cheese. In a jar add all dressing ingredients. Shake well and taste. Combine the cooled gyros strips, salad and dressing and coat well.

147.   **Chickpea And Edamame Salad**

Preparation time: 30 mins

Cooking time: 30 mins

Ingredient: 2 15.5oz each cans chickpea (garbanzo beans) rinsedand drained

3/4 cup edamame soy beans 1/3 cup chopped red pepper 1/3 cup chopped green pepper 1/4 cup diced carrots

3 tablespoons dried cranberries1 garlic clove minced Dressing

2 tablespoons grapeseed oil2 tablespoons olive oil

1 teaspoon white distilled vinegar1 teaspoon sugar

1/4 teaspoon dried oregano1/4 teaspoon dried basil

1/4 teaspoon dried rosemary

Salt and pepperDirections:

In a large bowl combine chickpeas, edamame, red pepper, green

pepper, carrots, dried cranberries, minced garlic and set aside. In a small bowl combine grapeseed oil, olive oil, vinegar, sugar, oregano, basil and rosemary. Whisk until blended. Pour dressing over chick peas and gently toss. Season with salt and pepper to taste. Chill for at least 30 minutes for flavors to blend. Serve chilled.

Flavour Boosters (Fish Glazes, Meat Rubs & Fish Rubs)

148.   Mexican Cocoa Rub

Want to spice up your dry meats with savory Mexican flavors? Try out my classy rub this weekend. Cocoa and espresso powder are a special addition to this Mexican style rub creating soothing spiced aroma.

Preparation Time: 5 min. Cooking Time: 5 min.
Servings: 9 tsp.

Ingredients:

Water – 1 tbs.

Cocoa, unsweetened – 1 tsp. Instant espresso powder – 2 tsp. Smoked paprika – 2 tsp.
Olive oil – 1 tsp. Ground cumin – 1 tsp. Salt – ¼ tsp.

Directions:

One by one, mix in all the ingredients in your mixing bowl to makethe cocoa rub. Gently mix all the ingredients using spatula or spoon to form an aromatic rub mixture.

Now, take your choice of meat cut and place it on a firm surface. Brush or rub the freshly made rub on it; pat gently for the rub to stick to the surface. Turn the meat cut and repeat to spice up its other side. Repeat with other meat cuts.

Let your meat cuts adequately season for more rich flavors for a few hours in your refrigerator. Take them out, as they are ready to be cooked or grilled!

149. Juniper Sage Meat Rub

This unique meat rub has been crafted with quality by including numerous healthy herbs such as juniper berries, lay leaf, red pepper,etc. It delivers piney accent to the rub, which ultimately enhances the flavor of your favorite meat cuts.

Preparation Time: 5 min.Cooking Time: 5 min. Servings: 8 tsp. Ingredients:

Bay leaf – 1 Black peppercorns - 1 tsp.Juniper berries - 2 tsp. Extra-virgin olive oil - 2 tbs. Crushed red pepper - ½ tsp.Kosher salt - ½ tsp.

Minced garlic – 1 cloveMinced sage leaves - 6Directions:

Mix in the bay leaf, red pepper, salt, peppercorns, and berries in yourspice blender, grinder or processor to make the juniper rub. Start processing or grinding the mixed spiced on "pulse" mode to ground.

Empty the mixed spice mixture in a bowl; mix in the sage leaves, oil, and garlic. Mix again well.

Now, take your choice of meat cut and place it on a firm surface. Brush or rub the freshly made rub on it; pat gently for the rub to stick to the surface. Turn the meat cut and repeat to spice up its other side. Repeat with other meat cuts.

The freshly rubbed meat is ready to be grilled or cooked!

Sauce Recipes

150.   Coconut Sugar Peanut Sauce

Preparation time: 5 minutes Cooking time: 5 minute
Servings: 1 ½ cups Ingredients

4 tablespoons coconut sugar

6 tablespoons powdered peanut butter 1 tablespoon chili
sauce

2 tablespoons liquid aminos

¼ cup of water

1 teaspoon lime juice

½ teaspoon ginger powderDirections:

In a bowl, combine all the ingredients until properly
combined. Serve

as a topping for the salad or other dishes.Store in a fridge.

Lightning Source UK Ltd.
Milton Keynes UK
UKHW021946140621
385519UK00002B/514